Power of Rituals

for Women

Power of Rituals

for Women

How to Connect, Cultivate and Celebrate the Relationships of Your Life

Linda Ann Smith and Kelly Blair Roberts

Power Publishing, Inc.
Aurora, Colorado

Power Publishing, Inc.
3765 So. Olathe Circle
Aurora, Colorado 80013

The instructions and advice in the book are not intended
as a substitute for psychological counseling. The authors and publisher
disclaim any responsibility or liability resulting from actions
advocated or discussed in this book. Those desiring or needing
psychological counseling are encouraged to seek the services of
competent professionals in that area of expertise.

Book Cover Design by F&B Graphic Design,
Rebecca Finkel, Ft. Collins, Colorado
www.fpgd.com
Illustrations: E.P. Puffin & Company,
Bobbie Shupe, Denver, Colorado
Interior Book Designer: WESType Publishing Services, Inc.
Ronnie Moore, Boulder, Colorado

Printed in Canada

Library of Congress Control Number: 2007928611

Power Publishing, Inc.
Power of Rituals for Women: How to connect, cultivate and celebrate
the relationships of your life/Linda Ann Smith and Kelly Blair Roberts
          p.   cm.
ISBN 978-0-9795846-0-2 (alk. Paper)
1. Ritual   2. Relationship   I. Title

1 2 3 4 5 6 7 8 9 10 11 12 13 14 15

This book is dedicated to my son Andrew Barnett Smith.
He was and will always be, the best part
of my whole life. The memory of his smile, laughter,
sweet heart, twinkling brown eyes and
the freckles sprinkled across his nose guides
and inspires me to bring rituals to the world.
The power of rituals helped me raise him and
helped me overcome his loss to be able
to create a life that has joy and meaning.

Linda Ann Smith

ENVIRONMENTAL BENEFITS STATEMENT

Power Publishing, Inc. saved the following resources by printing the pages of this book on chlorine free paper made with 100% post-consumer waste.

TREES	WATER	ENERGY	SOLID WASTE	GREENHOUSE GASES
22	7,880	15	1,012	1,898
FULLY GROWN	GALLONS	MILLION BTUs	POUNDS	POUNDS

Calculations based on research by Environmental Defense and the Paper Task Force. Manufactured at Friesens Corporation

Power Publishing, Inc. is committed to using green and sustainable products that lessen our impact on the environment.

Acknowledgments

"The reason one writes isn't the fact she wants to say something. She writes because she has something to say." ("He" in the original quote was replaced with "she").

—F. Scott Fitzgerald

Everyone has a book in them (see the ritual Author! Author!)—something to say about lessons learned in their life, the way they learned the lessons or the "aha" life changing moments. Kelly Blair Roberts and I had something to say about connecting, cultivating and celebrating relationships. Not only did we have something to say, but our friends and colleagues had something to say. This book went from dream status to reality with the support, cheering on, "aha" moments, ritual-testing and unconditional love from the relationships of our life.

Collaborating with a best friend on writing a book takes it into the big adventure sphere of experiences. Sharing a big adventure with Kelly Blair Roberts gave me the opportunity to share the belief in the power of rituals, the unbridled enthusiasm of people who participated in our rituals, the wordsmithing exercises and ritual-making with a best friend. Our big adventure was and continues to be a delightful journey. Kelly is the kind of best friend every woman should have. Her ability to listen, facilitate and then pour out just the right thing to say or write made it fun, easy and a celebration to write this book.

My ritual-resistant brothers, Larry (the elder) and Stephen (the baby), would macho-banter, tease and joke about the "R" word, but when the ritual started they brought their tender and sweet hearts into the process in a way that surprised and delighted. In the process of writing this book, their acceptance and their own ritual-making helped me keep my fingers on the keyboard. My father once said to me that I was the heart of the family. After bringing rituals to my family, the truth is that I facilitate my family's ability to bring their hearts into the family. Rituals in my family have provided healing through laughter and tears, but mostly the rituals have given us a way to connect to each other in a way that is life sustaining.

Our friends, too numerous to mention but you know who you are, contributed rituals, conducted their own, told us their stories, celebrated with us and have promised to buy at least ten books each to give as gifts to all of their other friends.

On a lighter note, I would like to acknowledge the Tattered Cover bookstore in Denver, Colorado which, when I went in search of a book like this one to create a 55th wedding anniversary ritual for my parents, did not have one on their bookshelves. This seemingly insignificant fact motivated me to call Kelly Blair Roberts from the store's pay phone and say "let's write a book on rituals!"

The writing of this book required testing each of the rituals, rather like testing recipes. In the testing, Kelly and I connected to each other and our relationships, we cultivated new relationships and we celebrated each and every one.

—Linda Ann Smith

What occurs to me as I acknowledge those who have traveled with us on our *Power of Rituals* journey is that this book would not exist were it not for the vision and commitment of my co-author Linda Ann Smith. She conceived it, drove the multi-faceted process of developing it and tapped professional expertise to enhance it. Most importantly, she believed in it even when other professional or personal responsibilities required our attention and drew us away. Linda was *always* there to rekindle our commitment and renew the itinerary for reaching our destination. Thanks, Linda, for your monumental drive.

Early on we wanted to invoke the support and input of our network of women friends. We converted the Quaker process of "Clearness Meetings" into a ritual (of course). Thanks to the guidance we received from our dear friends, we set our sights on writing the book and creating products to use with the rituals (we have several including the Baby Blessings ritual in the "Celebrations" chapter). And we have had our friends' support and guidance ever since—a good thing, because it takes a city to raise a book. Thanks, girlfriends, for your unswerving support and faith in us and the *Power of Rituals.*

We can't omit mentioning one of our networks, the Green Ladies, for their unique contribution. This group of women convened in the 90s based upon our common thread of environmental work. What began as a professional network has evolved over the years into a very personal one. Once a year since 1991, we Green Ladies have loaded up our cars with snowshoes and food for a weekend retreat at a cabin in Estes Park, Colorado. Our tradition of experiencing a ritual is a huge reason why we have stuck together and grown together. Given the spectrum of our life passages over the years, the annual ritual is a testament to the group's capacity to celebrate and support the gains and losses of the individual members. Thanks, Green Ladies, for the opportunity to experience the difference an annual ritual can make to the dynamism of a group.

I now know why so many authors attribute their success to an editor. We have been blessed with the contributions of three very skilled ones. Many versions of the book ago, we tapped Lisa Turner aka the Pink Diva to edit our compositions. Her style of including positive comments with the corrections made what could have been a scary process for two burgeoning authors into a love fest. Later on, we enlisted Sandy Widen, who helped launch one of Denver's most established weeklies, *The WestWord*, to put the book through her worldly filter. Her comments enabled us to fine tune the book for a larger audience. Our final editor Melanie Mulhall made our words sing, dance and get attention. Thank you, Lisa, Sandy and Melanie, for your shepherding us through this adventure.

I am thrilled to co-produce a book that has so much to offer our readers for connecting, cultivating and celebrating the relationships in their lives. I think that is what makes being human so special and what makes the world go around.

—Kelly Blair Roberts

Table of Contents

A New Meaning for Ritual

Rituals mean different things to people in different circumstances and cultures. For some, rituals are centered on religious ceremonies and functions. Others may associate rituals with cults. Yet there are rituals we all relate to as Americans. Consider sharing Valentine cards and gifts; hunting for Easter eggs; cheering for fireworks on the 4th of July; trick or treating for Halloween; and watching the parades for St. Patrick's Day, Memorial Day and Veterans Day. These are all rituals—they happen time and time again. We look forward to them, plan for them, and something is missing if we do not experience them every year. Another important aspect is that most of these experiences are created and done with families and friends.

Families, communities and religions have ancient rituals for births, weddings and end of life. Rituals are the foundation of cultural and family traditions. There are rituals unique to the Girl Scouts and the Boy Scouts, to corporate settings, civic groups and fraternal organizations. And there are smaller yet equally important rituals: celebrating the birth of a new baby, a veteran snapping to attention when "Taps" is played as a comrade-in-arms is laid to rest, a touch football game after Thanksgiving dinner.

Americans are living differently since 9/11. A *CNN/USA Today* Gallup poll conducted shortly after the tragedy found that the terrorist attack was a life altering experience for more than one-third of Americans. More than half of those surveyed said it compelled them to spend more time with family and friends. The aftermath of 9/11 brought a renewed sense that connection is the path for Americans to overcome the sense of vulnerability that has woven its way into the fabric of our lives.

This book creates a new meaning for the world *ritual* providing transformational experiences for your relationships. The rituals you will find between the covers of our book:

Have:
❖ A start and a finish
❖ A structured recipe or process
❖ An intention
❖ A desired result

Are:

- ❖ Structured yet dynamic and fluid
- ❖ Religion neutral
- ❖ Fun

Can Become:

- ❖ Customs
- ❖ Traditions
- ❖ Cherished activities and memories
- ❖ Defining moments in your life and relationships

Are not:

- ❖ Random acts
- ❖ Religious Ceremonies
- ❖ "Hokey" or "touchy feely" (unless you want them to be)

Power of Rituals for Women is written for women and their friends and family who want to laugh, tease, argue, advise, encourage, inspire and believe that women are a girl's best friend.

As women, connected to a family and community, we learn profound lessons about values, honor, truth and dignity from the stories we hear from others and the time we spend together.

"The connections between and among women are . . .
the most potentially transforming force on the planet."
—Adrienne Rich
(Poet and theorist in the contemporary women's movement)

Take note of how many people walk and talk on their cell phone, drive and talk, work out and talk, sit in coffee shops and talk. The need to be connected and stay connected is a fundamental human need.

Rituals are the glue that binds us together as families, as friends, as communities. And in a world in which we seek to stay connected with what is truly important, we need the power of rituals today more than ever.

Rituals give *power* to relationships. Creating, cultivating and celebrating human connection is the premise of our books. Rituals create connections through clear intentions and activities. The rituals in this book honor the significant, as well as the simple moments of our lives so we can learn from those moments and pass on our knowledge. Rituals provide safe havens in times of heartache and loss, as well as being conduits for celebrating joy and prosperity.

Power of Rituals for Women is the first book in a series offering new meaning to rituals—rituals that have power for enriching our human connections. The rituals in this book are drawn from the experiences of women sharing their life experiences, supporting each other and celebrating each other's significant passages. Women do this naturally and in many cases without much conscious effort. Ask any woman if she has a cherished group of women friends and chances are there is an activity they do on a regular basis. Oprah often speaks about her rituals with her best friend Gayle. The *Sex in the City* girlfriends met regularly over meals to dissect every nuance of being single in New York City . . . and, of course, shoe shopping (see the Shoe-Shopping Good or Shoe'n Tell Ritual in the "Just for Fun" chapter). The authors take a yearly weekend snow-shoeing trip with the same group of women and conduct the much-anticipated Saturday Night Ritual.

We want to hear about your rituals with your cherished women friends, family, co-workers, children or just yourself. Go to www.PowerofRituals.com and share your rituals so that others may be inspired by you to connect, cultivate and celebrate the extraordinary relationships of their lives.

About the Authors

The Story of Co-Author Linda Ann Smith

My women friends stood beside me as I buried my son. They then helped me learn how to live again through the unspeakable grief of a mother's shattered life and heart. As friends they stood with me in my pain. As mothers they felt my pain. As women they helped ease my pain. Without my friends, I would not have been able to find a pathway back into a life where I was able to experience joy.

I was inspired to write a book on rituals when I needed an idea for a 55th wedding anniversary celebration for my parents. Their anniversary came just seven months after I lost my only son in a car crash. I had created rituals to raise my son, strengthen bonds with my family, enrich relationships with my girlfriends and just to have a good time. However, my creativity was crushed under the intense grief of losing Andrew. I found no book at the bookstore with rituals to use or adapt for the anniversary. At first, not finding a book made me impatient. Then, struck by a brainstorm, I called Kelly Blair Roberts, one of my best friends, with the idea to write the book. It was a big first step to opening my self into a life of extraordinary possibilities.

Growing up with brothers, I always yearned for a sister. In lieu of a sister, I had legions of girlfriends. Girlfriends who would say "poor baby" when I needed it, kick me in the butt to get me out of a funk, help me (move, paint, organize garage sales) and love me unconditionally. When I need the truth, I turn to my women friends. The rituals that Kelly and I have done with our friends are the foundation of *Power of Rituals for Women.* I have been transformed by the power of my friends.

The Story of Co-Author Kelly Blair Roberts

I met my first best friend in kindergarten. We were inseparable and shared the rituals of early girlhood—spending the night together, dressing up in our mothers' clothes and jewelry and making believe we were grown-ups. Our Sunday morning ritual consisted of a breakfast of scrambled eggs and those cinnamon rolls that come in a can with a smaller can of frosting inside. Unlike my family, her family always had leftover rolls. I could eat as many as I wanted. I can't imagine life without girlfriends and the rituals we share—or life without cinnamon rolls, either.

Seasons and Holidays

"Celebrate the happiness that friends are always giving,
Make every day a holiday and celebrate just living."
—**Amanda Bradley, Poet**

Word by Word

I love it when a ritual comes together! As a guest at a dinner party where I knew the women, I couldn't resist bringing along a ritual in honor of a New Year with its bright possibilities. Somewhere in my travels I picked up polished stones with one word inscribed on each stone. For this ritual, I used the stones as prompters for each woman to relate her hopes and dreams for the New Year.

The stones were placed inscribed side down and we each selected one without knowing the word engraved on it. Then we each used the word on our stone to fashion a story that illuminated our hopes and intentions for the coming year.

The dinner was wonderful, all the more so because of the shared stories accompanying the shared meal. In fact, we discovered that stories can be better than food—they nourished us with a banquet of possibilities that inspired us all.

—Linda Ann Smith

Purpose

❖ Celebrate and share lessons learned, intentions for the New Year, and hopes and dreams.

Props

- Stones inscribed with a word, or pieces of paper with one word written on each. These are the words inscribed on the stones I used: Harmony, Succeed, Imagine, Wonder, Share, Hope, Wisdom, Romance, Risk, Dream, Learn.
- A timer or watch with a second hand (to avoid a filibuster).

Presentation

- Put the stones or slips of paper in a basket and pass the basket so each person can choose one.
- Ask each person to share her hopes, dreams and intention for the New Year, based on the word she chose.
- Agree how much time to allow for each person. Anyone who is sharing from the heart can easily become caught up in telling her story and lose track of time.

Other Ways to Go

- Try this ritual for birthdays, anniversaries, job promotions, career moves, new home purchases. Choose words that are appropriate to the occasion as well as wildly inappropriate to add a little fun to the ritual.
- Give each person five slips of paper and ask her to write one word on each. Use these words for the ritual.

Burning Desires

Remember Benjamin Bratt? Julia Roberts' Benjamin Bratt? On some talk show right after the holidays, in some year in the not so distant past, Benjamin told of a ritual Julia did on New Year's Eve.

Julia asked her guests to write a wish or intention for the New Year and share it with everyone. Then each guest deposited the slip into her fireplace in which a fire was blazing. There it would be released as positive energy into the universe, increasing the chances that the wish would be brought to fruition in the New Year.

As Benjamin told the story, I was struck by his delight in performing the ritual. That is what has lingered. There is so much hope for men in the ritual department—just ask my ritual-resistant brothers, who have become converts!

—Linda Ann Smith

Purpose

❖ Connect and share lessons learned, your intention for the New Year and your hopes and dreams.

Props

- ❖ A fireplace with a stoked fire. If a fireplace is not available, use a large metal bowl. Please take appropriate safety precautions when performing this ritual.
- ❖ Slips of paper and pens for everyone.

Presentation

- ❖ Ask your guests to write their intentions, hopes or dreams for the New Year on the slip of paper or, if they have more than one, on several slips of paper.
- ❖ Take turns sharing what you wrote. Allow others to offer comments and support.
- ❖ Ceremoniously toss the slip of paper into the fireplace. If you are using a bowl, strike the match when all the slips of paper are in the bowl. Make sure there is a pitcher of water next to the bowl, as a precaution against flare-ups.

Halloween with Heroines

Who would you pick as your all time favorite heroine and how would you spend an evening in her shoes?

As defined by the *Standard College Dictionary*, a heroine performs brave deeds, showing great daring or boldness. Heroines have always been important to me, whether in real life, in movies or in books. As a girl, I was enthralled by the adventures of Nancy Drew. As I entered the workforce, I benefited from the presence of women mentors who helped me to succeed . . . my real life heroines.

For example, Joey was my supervisor at a family owned business. Outwardly, we could not have been more different. She always dressed to kill in fashionable suits and high, high heels, in contrast to my blue jean bell-bottoms and clunky shoes. In spite of our differences, we had an affinity. She assigned projects that required me to stretch and learn. Her support was so effective that when she moved out of state, I took her place coordinating the company's advertising programs.

Other heroines in my life are women I don't know personally, but whose presence in the world has a positive impact on my life. For instance, I have always admired Jane Fonda for her courage to stand up for what she believes, even if it means being criticized—a trait I'm still trying to grow into.

Other women I view as heroines are not famous. They are ordinary women doing extraordinary work. Carolyn Jaffe, co-founder of the Hospice of Metro Denver, is such a woman. She made it possible for thousands of terminal patients to die peacefully at home before she died her own peaceful death in 2001.

Paola Gianturco and Toby Tuttle, who wrote the book, *In Her Hands: Craftswomen Changing the World,* tell the stories of indigenous craftswomen from around the world making traditional handicrafts to keep their children alive and provide them with schooling. They write, "We had a purpose—to shine a light on these *invisible heroines,* to give them a little of the glory they so richly deserve."

This ritual provides the opportunity for women to spend Halloween dressed up as their favorite heroines.

—Kelly Blair Roberts

Purpose

❖ Celebrate the power of women and their impact on the world in a lighthearted way.

Props

❖ Invitations explaining the purpose and the dress code.
❖ Location for the party.
❖ Your own heroine costume.
❖ Drinks and table settings for the potluck.

Preparation

❖ Identify the women you want to be part of this Halloween event.

❖ Send out invitations asking that each woman come dressed as her favorite heroine (a woman who has made her mark on the world) and be prepared to share her heroine's story.

❖ Have the guests bring a refreshment that her heroine might bring to a potluck.

Presentation

❖ As the guests arrive, ask each guest to postpone revealing her heroine for a time and, instead, to interact with the other guests as her heroine might—in terms of how she might act and what she might talk about.

❖ When everyone has had time to talk and eat, ask them to take a seat. Pass out a list of questions and sentences to complete and tell guests they will be answering any three of them, each using the words and attitudes of her heroine. (Let them know that it is okay to make up the answers if they are unsure what their heroine would say.)

❖ Take turns, with each guest answering.

❖ Some possible questions/sentences to complete for the list:

> What has been your greatest personal challenge?
>
> What physical trait do you like about yourself and why?
>
> What is your unrelenting passion?
>
> What is the best gift you have ever given?
>
> I love it when people say . . .
>
> A hallelujah moment for me was when . . .
>
> What is the memory that *always* makes you smile?
>
> What teacher inspired you? How?
>
> Tell a story of how you became the person you are today.
>
> What is your most endearing quality?
>
> What is the best gift you ever received?
>
> My biggest fear is . . .
>
> Describe your perfect day.
>
> The life lesson that changed my life was . . .

❖ After each guest speaks on behalf of her heroine, ask the others if they can guess the heroine's identity.

❖ Have the guest explain why this woman is her heroine and how that heroine has made her mark on the world.

❖ After all the heroines have been revealed, ask everyone to answer this question:

> What did you learn or find surprising about each other and your heroines?

Other Ways To Go

❖ Pick a specific genre and ask the guests to come as: their favorite actresses, philanthropists, world leaders, local celebrities, etc.

❖ To celebrate a birthday, have each guest come as one of the birthday woman's qualities.

"The first ritual I participated in was the ***Feed Your Inner Poet*** ritual (page 90) during a family Thanksgiving dinner. I am a typical American male, always consciously protective of my inner me. I was also a little leery of the word 'ritual' and how it was going to be. However, it was family and I was committed to giving it a try because family is very important to me.

The ritual was a fun and creative way to share and learn from and about others in the family. The ritual helped reveal new and delightful information about each other. A ritual as a tool for strengthening bonds is invaluable and something I am thankful for having been introduced to. Being able to connect with my family in a fun and creative way cultivated a memory and experience I will long cherish."

—Brian White, Brand Marketing Executive

Holidaze Time Out

I love Christmas: the colorful blinking strands of lights, evergreen boughs with red bows, the smell of baking cookies, lovingly decorated trees indoors and out, special gatherings and familiar seasonal music. On the other hand, this season can be overwhelmingly busy, which is why I've dubbed it the *holildaze*. I created this ritual to give myself and my friends a respite to relax and focus on our inner selves during a season with so many external activities.

—Kelly Blair Roberts

Purpose

❖ Cultivate relaxation and reflection. As a whole life coach, I believe every one of us has something unique and special to offer the world. And I see how understanding this makes a difference in the lives of my clients. Use this ritual to gain clarity about your gifts to the world.

Props

❖ A pen.
❖ A specially purchased candle.
❖ A greeting card, envelope and stamp.
❖ A few minutes of solitude.
❖ A place to be comfortable and uninterrupted.
❖ Music.

Presentation

- ❖ Some time during the holidaze, take a few minutes for yourself in a comfortable setting.
- ❖ Light your candle and play your music.
- ❖ Pose this question to yourself: What is the special gift I bring to the world?
- ❖ Once you are clear you have the answer, write it in the greeting card.
- ❖ Address the card and mail it to yourself.
- ❖ As the New Year unfolds, refer to this card and burn this candle to remind you of the gift you bring to the world.

Other Ways to Go

- ❖ This ritual could just as easily be done with a group. The presentation remains the same except for an additional step in which the participants share and explore how to support each other in bringing out their unique gifts to the world.

Thankfully Thanksgiving

Thanksgiving is all about food, football, family and—let's not forget—thanks. We have all participated in the ritual of telling what we are thankful for. My family will forever be on the top of my personal thankful list. I have always felt loved and cherished by them and their ability to make me laugh, cry, scream and stomp my feet in total frustration has made my life whole and interesting.

My mother's holiday dinners are legendary in my family. She is famous for her innocent double entendre one-liners that made her blush when pointed out—and make for enduring Thanksgiving stories. She is also famous for the memorable Thanksgiving when someone made the mistake of giving her a martini before dinner was served. That martini turned her into a football quarterback with a bad passing arm. When she served the mashed potatoes, the bowl went flying across the table into someone's lap.

Sending food flying has become an occasional Thanksgiving quirk in our family, if not an actual tradition. Once, when my Uncle Jimmy got a little exuberant while telling a story, his Italian flying hand connected with a pie and sent it sailing across the room.

My memories of our family dinners are filled with laughter and the essence of belonging. Below are ideas for you and your family and friends to give thanks for your treasure chest of relationships.

—Linda Ann Smith

Purpose

❖ Celebrate thanks at Thanksgiving.

Props

❖ Thanksgiving dinner

Presentations (choose as many as you like)

❖ Ask each person at the table to pick out one or more people present at table and thank him/her/them for something specific that they did, said, influenced or supported in the recent—or not so recent—past.

❖ Thanksgiving memory recall: Ask everyone to recall memories of Thanksgivings past.

❖ Ask each person to come with a letter, written beforehand to another dinner guest, thanking that person for something specific. Ask each recipient to read his/her letter at the table.

❖ Create a Thanksgiving story, either true or fictitious. Start with a beginning sentence to the story. Go around the table and ask each person to add to the story. Tape recording this would be fun. Here are a few suggestions for story starters:

> I called my mother the week before Thanksgiving to tell her . . .

> As I was driving toward home for the Thanksgiving holiday, there appeared on the side of the road . . .

When the door opened on Thanksgiving morning . . .
What is it about pumpkin pie that . . .

❖ Honor and thank your ancestors: Set the table with pieces inherited from your forbearers and then ask each person to give their memory of the ancestor and characteristics they believe the ancestor possessed.

❖ Ask parents and others to tell stories and memories of your grandparents, uncles, great uncles—as far back as they can go.

❖ Relate to your family. What characteristics and personality traits do you possess that are like those of your mother, grandmother or father. For instance, I have my father's trait of being obsessively organized, his tenacity, and his eyes. I have my mother's hands, her hair and her quick temper. (I wish I had her artistic ability.) Let others at the table tell what they see in you or themselves that relates to your living family members and ancestors.

❖ Try the Feed Your Inner Poet ritual in the "Just for Fun" chapter. Write a collective poem about Thanksgiving, this particular Thanksgiving or another Thanksgiving that everyone at the table has a memory about.

❖ What does family mean to you? Ask this question of everyone at the table. What are the rights, obligations, joys, privileges or burdens of family?

❖ Use the *Dinner Talk Cards*© (available at www.PowerofRituals.com) or develop your own set of Dinner Talk Cards that relate to your family or friends and Thanksgiving. Pass the bowl of questions around the table and let the fun begin.

❖ Create a family cookbook. Ask guests to bring their favorite recipes (children too), along with photos of themselves and, if they really want to get creative, photos of the dishes to accompany the recipes. Set up a table with art supplies and pages for the cookbook. Conduct a family scrapbooking event around the photos and the recipes. Encourage people to not just provide recipes, but write a little about them, too.

Okay, that was fun—now, how about a game of touch football?

Mama Mia

The late humorist, Erma Bombeck, once suggested that a mother is born when a child enters this world through the birth canal. I like the point she makes about women being born into motherhood. It is a role not taught, but learned— through *years* of trial and error. Given the relentless responsibilities of being a mom, I created this ritual for not just a day, but a weekend, of pampering, pleasantries and surprises.

The idea for giving your mom a gift certificate to a spa is heartily endorsed by my co-author Linda, otherwise known as the Spa Queen. She manages to get massages in more places than most people can imagine, let alone have the opportunity to visit.

—Kelly Blair Roberts

Purpose

❖ Celebrate an unforgettably special Mother's Day (weekend).

Props

❖ A gift certificate for a day spa.
❖ A family dinner on Mother's Day at Mom's favorite restaurant, or at a house other than her own.

❖ Questions/sentences to complete from the *Dinner Talk Cards©* (available at www.PowerofRituals.com) that family members answer in advance of the dinner. (See samples below.)

❖ A bouquet of flowers or a corsage.

❖ Mother's Day cards.

Preparation

❖ Contact family members well in advance of Mother's Day to ask for their support and donations for the gift certificate.

❖ Decide whether to hold the family dinner at someone's home and, if so, what dishes will be cooked by whom or make reservations at the restaurant.

❖ Purchase a gift certificate to a local spa.

❖ Decide on the *Dinner Talk Cards©* questions/sentences to complete. (See samples below.)

❖ Distribute the questions/sentences to complete to family members in advance so they have time to come up with their answers. Ask everyone to write their favorite answer in a Mother's Day card.

❖ Mail the (surprise) gift certificate to your mom, along with an invitation to dinner on Mother's Day. Be sure to send it off in plenty of time for her to receive it and make an appointment for the Saturday before Mother's Day and reserve Mother's Day evening for your dinner.

❖ Depending on your mom's preference, buy her a bouquet of flowers or a corsage.

Presentation

❖ Assemble for the family dinner either at someone's home or at the restaurant and present your mom with her flowers or corsage.

❖ Over the course of the meal, take turns sharing your answers to the *Dinner Talk Cards*© questions/sentences to complete.

❖ After everyone has shared their answers, ask your mom to finish this sentence: What I appreciate most about being the mother in this family is . . .

❖ Present her with the Mother's Day cards to take home as reminders of her Mama Mia status with your family.

Sample Questions/Sentences to Complete

(Listed here are sample questions/sentences to complete from the collection of *Dinner Talk Cards*© that are a product of the *Power of Rituals*. You can order your set of cards online at www.PowerofRituals.com.)

❖ The funniest memory I have of Mom is . . .

❖ My favorite physical trait that I have of Mom's is . . .

❖ Have I ever told you about the time that Mom . . .

❖ A family tradition of Mom's that I treasure the most is . . .

❖ The best gift I ever received from Mom is . . .

❖ The quality I most admire about Mom is . . .

❖ My earliest memory of Mom is . . .

❖ My favorite saying of Mom's is . . .

❖ The personal quality of Mom's that I wish I had is . . .

❖ Mom's theme song would be . . .

Other Ways to Go

❖ This ritual can be adapted for birthdays, anniversaries and other celebrations by choosing questions/sentences to complete from the *Dinner Talk Cards©* that complement the occasion.

Ideas for Rituals for Seasons & Holidays

OCCASION #1:

_____

_____

Name of ritual and page number to use as a guide

_____

Ideas to create connections with the people in your life

_____

Ideas to cultivate old memories or new ones

_____

Ideas to celebrate people or special occasions

_____

_____

OCCASION #2:

_____

_____

Name of ritual and page number to use as a guide

_____

Ideas to create connections with the people in your life

_____

Ideas to cultivate old memories or new ones

_____

Ideas to celebrate people or special occasions

_____

_____

Celebrations

"I have used rituals on many celebratory occasions to honor my family and friends. These rituals have never failed to serve as a catalyst toward creating strong, warm and more intimate connections between the participants. We have always come away with new, and at times, extraordinary insight into ourselves as well as others. This has been accomplished in very creative and enthralling ways so even the shy or skeptical are willing to participate. Under the guise of fun, many doors of enlightenment have been opened."

—**Kathy Filgo, Writer, Fine Lines, Inc.,**
Genesee, Colorado

Memories are Made of this

"Winters must be very cold for people who have no warm memories." Deborah Kerr soulfully utters these words to Cary Grant in *An Affair to Remember* as they gaze at the site of their destiny—the Empire State Building. Memories are the glue that holds friends, families, and communities together. Sharing warm memories holds as much or more richness than creating the memories.

I created this ritual as a Christmas gift for my parents-who-have-everything one year. Everyone in the family received pages of a journal with instructions to write an individual memory on the page as well as paint, draw or attach photos on their page. The completed pages were returned to me and I put them in a journal. During our family Christmas dinner, we passed the journal around and took turns reading other people's memories. It was a long dinner as one memory sparked another one. The holiday had a special glow that year from re-connecting to our history as a family. The response from our parents: "The best gift of all!"

—Linda Ann Smith

Purpose

❖ Celebrate a significant event and cultivate memories.

Props

❖ Journal with plenty of detachable pages for the size of your family or group.

Presentation

❖ Invitations to guests including a journal page or two with instructions on completing and returning in plenty of time to create the finished journal.

❖ Include specifics of the event: who is being honored, time, place and date.

❖ During dinner or at an appropriate time, pass the journal around and take turns reading the memories, yours or someone elses. Allow time for other memories to spring forth.

❖ Provide refreshments or dinner during the memory sharing.

❖ Close the ritual by presenting the journal to the honoree(s). This may be a good time to ask the honoree(s) to share a few of their own memories.

Other Ways To Go

❖ Try this ritual for anniversaries, a child's graduation or moving from one home to another.

❖ Check out the book *Stop Screaming at the Microwave* by Mary LoVerde. (www.maryloverde.com) for other ideas of capturing and honoring your memories.

Baby Blessings

Newborn babies create the best opportunity for a ritual. This ritual was created for my niece Alison's first son, McKenzie. McKenzie was not at all impressed with the ritual. His screaming is heard throughout the recording of the event and most of the pictures show a very unhappy baby with a red scrunched face and mouth wide open. However, I know he will cherish this book as he grows older.

I finally made my second great-nephew's memory book nine years after he was born. My niece tells me that he keeps it by his bed to read nightly.

—Linda Ann Smith

Purpose

❖ Celebrate the arrival of a new baby and create a memory book for the baby.

Props

❖ Digital camera (ability to print the photos at the party is a plus).

❖ Tape recorder with blank tape.

❖ Postcards.

❖ Pens or colored markers.

❖ Scrapbook album.

❖ Scrapbooking supplies: stamps, stickers, buttons.
Inform guests beforehand what you are doing and ask
them to bring their own treasures to include in the
memory book for the baby. I used the Creative
Memories scrapbooking technique. You will find
more information at www.creativememories.com.
Memory book supplies can also be found at any crafts
or scrapbook store.

Presentation

❖ Invite the baby and his/her parents, as well as family
and friends. Let them know that this is a special
occasion to bless and welcome the baby into the
family and extended family.
❖ Gather everyone around the baby.
❖ Ask each person to hold the baby for a photo.
❖ Tape record a wish for the baby from the person
holding the baby and ask them to write the wish on a
decorative postcard after passing the baby to the next
well-wisher.
❖ The host can create an album with the photos and
wishes or all the supplies can be available at the
celebration for each person to create her own page for
the album with her photo. Creating the album on the
spot may not necessitate photo printing capabilities at
the site of the event, but that capability certainly
heightens the experience.

❖ This is the baby's book. S/he may not only learn to read with it, but will probably also refer to it with embarrassment as a teen, with comfort as a young adult and with awe when her/his own children arrive. And, in all likelihood, s/he will cherish it enough to want to give the same gift to the next generation.

❖ Oh, and take photos of everyone creating her page for the baby's memory book.

"Of all of the joys that lighten suffering earth, what joy is welcomed like a new-born child."

—Caroline Norton, Author early 1800's

Is there a new baby on the way in your circle of friends or family? Your answers to these questions will help you customize a baby blessing ritual for the expectant parents.

What values are important to the parents?

_____

_____

What rituals from their religious or ethnic background do they value?

_____

Are there family ancestors the parents want to honor by instilling their values in the life of their child?

_____

_____

What family and friends do the parents want to be actively involved in the child's life?

_____

_____

What information or wishes would the parents like to capture from friends and family to keep for the child?

_____

_____

What type of memorabilia would the parents like to have as a result of the baby blessing ritual?

_____

_____

Spa Bridal Shower

I would like to suggest that all of the rituals in this book or any of the *Power of Rituals* books can be done in a spa. My dad used to say that he enjoyed beer all over the world and never had a bad bottle of beer. I say the same thing about spas. I have partaken in the joys of spas from Nairobi to England, from California to New York, from Canada to Mexico and I have never been in a bad spa.

Not at all surprising, about one out of three times I am luxuriating at a spa, there is a group of women celebrating the upcoming nuptials of one of their own by spending the day being pampered at said spa.

Now, although you can most definitely spend your entire time at the spa being rubbed, moisturized, exfoliated, steamed and painted, this is a prime opportunity to offer your betrothed girlfriend a memorable ritual. As her friend, giving her something to sustain her through the wild ride of wedding planning, the wedding day, the honeymoon and the first few months of connubial bliss will be better than . . . I was going to say the spa experience but, NOT!

—Linda Ann Smith

Purpose

❖ Celebrate and connect to the bride.

Presentation Ideas

❖ Create a "girlfriend" bouquet. Ask everyone participating in the spa wedding shower to bring a silk flower with a little card tied to it bearing a wish, sage advice or even a short story of her experience with weddings or marriage.

❖ Chip in to purchase a spectacular crystal vase for the flower arrangement that will, no doubt, have a place of honor in the bride's new home.

❖ During a break in the pampering, gather around cups of tea and/or wine. Read your cards to the bride. Let others add their comments to your reading.

❖ Or, write a collective poem about marriage.

◆ Provide a list of must-use words on little slips of paper from which the shower guests will draw. Use words pertaining to weddings and marriage, but also words that have no connection at all—for instance *coffee, laundromat, Mississippi.*

◆ Each guest draws 5-10 words.

◆ One guest acts as the facilitator for writing the poem but everyone participates. The facilitator may, for instance, provide the format to be used and suggest a first line or stanza with each guest then adding a line or stanza. Alternatively, it might be fun to collaborate as a group on the entire poem, using the words each guest has picked.

◆ Once the poem is written, ask the bride to read it.

◆ One of the guests takes responsibility for producing it in a format, perhaps framed, so it can be presented to the bride on her first anniversary.

❖ Before you leave, schedule a six-month anniversary ritual at the spa.

"The more you praise and celebrate your life, the more there is in life to celebrate."

—Oprah Winfrey

Reunions Are Not Always Relative

Family reunions will be covered in depth in our book *Power of Rituals for Families*. Here, we are addressing the myriad other reunions that happen throughout the world, including reunions of college roommates, support groups, neighbors, and business colleagues.

Kelly and I have been part of a women's support group called the Green Ladies. We christened our group with this name because, at the beginning of our friendship in 1992, all ten of us were in environmental careers spanning government, corporate and nonprofit venues. We bonded over waste, trash, compost, recycling, water conservation and, of course, the politics of saving the planet. Over the years there have been a few changes. Some members are no longer in environmental careers but still live an environmentally friendly life.

Every winter we reunite at Valhalla Resort's Cabin 20 in Estes Park, Colorado. The agenda has not altered one iota over the years. Some arrive on Friday night; the rest on Saturday morning. We ceremoniously load the refrigerator and cupboards with the food we will joyfully prepare and enjoy together. Saturday afternoon is spent snowshoeing—or, in the occasional drought year, hiking—in our beloved, beautifully pristine Rocky Mountain National Park. And come evening, we gather around the fire and food for a reunion ritual. This Saturday evening ritual cements our bond, changes our lives, puts us back on track and leaves no question that we are supported, loved and honored by each other for who we are and what we do in the world.

The following ritual, *Lighting the World,* is one we conducted to honor other women we know who are changing the world.

—Linda Ann Smith

Purpose

❖ Celebrate women who have changed the world or "light" the world in a special or unique way.

Props

❖ Candles (another ritual with candles. No chanting, but if you feel moved to chant, please do!)

Presentation

❖ Place all of the candles in the middle of the table on a fire-proof platter. There should be one candle for each woman present. (As with other rituals using candles, have a pitcher of water close at hand.)

❖ Ask each women to talk about an absent women friend, including the work that woman is doing in the world and why it is important for everyone present.

❖ Light the candle in the woman's honor.

❖ Close the ritual by acknowledging each other for the work you are doing in the world.

❖ Each participant later informs the woman she chose to honor, sharing with her what was said, and presenting her with the candle.

Other Ways To Go

❖ Reunions of female friends are times to practice self-care. If you belong to a women's group, check in with each member to see if there is a particular focus that would benefit everyone. For instance, the "Write'n Hike" ritual in the "Telling Stories" chapter would be a great ritual to do for a women's group reunion. Design the story prompts for issues and life challenges with which the members are dealing. If you need help with this contact us at info@PowerOfRituals.com.

❖ Make your time together a time to share and support each other. A three-part theme could be "What I did last year, what I want to do next year and what help I need." This does not need to be a major undertaking. It can be a simple as creating balance in your life. Create a safe place for the sharing. For instance: offer only positive feedback; avoid interrupting the person sharing, yet set a length of time for their sharing so others also have an opportunity to share; make confidentiality a prerequisite, and; allow the emotional space for tears and laughter.

❖ The reunion could also include the sharing or exchange of unwanted clothing, handbags and/or jewelry. Set up a room where everything can be displayed and tried on. Some of my favorite outfits have come from friends.

❖ We would be remiss if we did not suggest holding your reunion of women friends at your favorite spa! Create time between the pampering appointments for sitting out on the deck and having mini-rituals. Any ritual in this book could be reformatted into a fifteen-minute mini-ritual.

❖ Reunions are about telling stories and hearing the stories of the others in your life you cherish and hold dear. Create a storytelling time, space and structure and it will transform the time you spend at your reunion.

Birthday Buy the Book

"Literature is my Utopia."

—Helen Keller

"There is more treasure in books than in all the pirate's loot on Treasure Island."

—Walt Disney

I cannot imagine going through childhood, or life for that matter, without books. They are my bridge from daylight to nocturnal realities. I read myself to sleep every night.

My parents were avid readers so, as a family, we were regular patrons of the public library. To this day, the musty smell of books triggers fond memories of summer afternoons in the library of my youth.

If you are a book lover, this ritual is right up your alley—or should I say aisle?

—Kelly Blair Roberts

Purpose

❖ Celebrate a birthday with books connecting to the birthday woman's passions and interests.

Props

❖ Invitations.
❖ Bookplates and glue.

❖ Large gift bag.
❖ Birthday cake, birthday candles, napkins, knife and forks.

Preparation

❖ Gain the cooperation of a friendly bookstore—preferably the birthday woman's favorite—at which to hold the party.
❖ Ask the birthday woman when she would like to celebrate her birthday and with whom.
❖ Draw up a list of the birthday woman's passions and interests. Provide as many as there are invitees.
❖ Send out invitations explaining the ritual and assign one of the passions or interests to each invitee (matching the interest to the invitee when possible).
❖ Call the bookstore to let them know the date and time that a buying party will take place and to arrange for a space in the store with comfortable seating for your party.
❖ Prepare bookplates that can be pasted into the front of a book for each invitee using rectangles of heavy paper with:

To:
From:
Why I Chose This Book for You:

❖ Make or purchase a birthday cake the day of the party.

Presentation

- ❖ Gather at the pre-arranged location in the bookstore.
- ❖ Ask the birthday woman to share her wishes and dreams for the next year of her life.
- ❖ Explain that each guest has thirty minutes to look for a book to purchase that connects with the passion or interest they were assigned.
- ❖ Encourage the birthday woman to look for a book that connects with what she is hoping for during the next year.
- ❖ While everyone is shopping, prepare to serve the cake.
- ❖ Reassemble after everyone has returned with their books and present the cake. Have the birthday woman make her wish and blow out the candles, then serve the cake.
- ❖ Take turns presenting the books, with each presenter explaining which of the birthday woman's passions or interests she has been charged with finding a book to represent and how the chosen book connects with it. (If the birthday woman already owns the book, she can exchange it for another of her choosing.)
- ❖ After each guest has presented her book, distribute the bookplates for them to sign and paste into the book she chose (making sure, of course, to separate any book to be exchanged from the stack of books to be book-plated).

❖ Make a list of the titles and authors to share with everyone by e-mail in the near future. Put all the books being kept in the gift bag and make a separate stack of books to be exchanged.

❖ Ask the birthday woman to share what book she chose for herself and how she hopes both it and those chosen for her will make her life richer in the upcoming year.

Other Ways to Go

❖ Rather than meeting at the bookstore, arrange to meet in someone's home. Ask everyone to buy their books in advance and bring them to the party. Everything else remains the same.

❖ Select a book you would like all of the guests to read in common. Compile a guest list, complete with names and addresses and room below or to the right of each name for that person to comment. Include your own name and address at the end of the list so it comes full circle. Send the book to the first person on the list with a note to send it on to the next person on the list once she has read it. At the top of the recipients' list, ask everyone to comment on the book, in the space provided below or next to their name. In this way, women living in different parts of the country or world can be part of a virtual book club.

The Wrinkle Ritual

The following was written by the sixteen year old daughter of a good friend of the co-authors. We think she states the case for wrinkles beautifully, and it is heartening to find such maturity and depth in such a young woman. We suspect that she will host her own wrinkle rituals as her internal beauty lengthens and her exterior beauty is enhanced by a few life affirming wrinkles.

—Linda Ann Smith & Kelly Blair Roberts

According to this culture's aesthetic laws, growing older is a disgraceful thing; something to be avoided for years with anti-wrinkle cream and then eventually fixed with face lifts and liposuction. But is there not a certain beauty to every moment that caused deep laugh lines? Or perhaps even the times of strife that caused a mouth to turn down at the corners? Many women, and, indeed, some men, find as they grow older, their allure—perhaps the natural smoothness and tautness of skin, or maybe the well-toned muscles of younger years—dissolves, leaving behind a mask of a past glamour. It is the sadness of this culture that youth equates beauty.

But there is a beauty to all women who decide that their money is better spent on charity than plastic surgery. Wrinkles are the reminders of a previous life, a vital and everlasting thing that starts in the 40s and simply get longer and deeper as emotion adds up over the years and the soul becomes complete by the time the person's life is over.

—Kristin Kudebeh - 9/04/06

Purpose

❖ Celebrate life stories.

Props

❖ Hand mirror.

Presentation

❖ Behold your lovely face in the hand mirror.
❖ Share your stories represented by the wonderful wrinkles: the laugh lines that were a gift from the joys of your life, the worry lines earned from the experiences that taught you the hardest life lessons, and the wrinkles earned through living your life with integrity, making the tough but right decisions that had the power to bring you to your knees.
❖ Close the ritual by creating a poem together—each woman adds one line to the poem.
❖ Ask for a volunteer to make copies of the poem and distribute them to the women.

Ideas for Rituals for Celebrations

OCCASION #1:

_____

_____

Name of ritual and page number to use as a guide

_____

Ideas to create connections with the people in your life

_____

Ideas to cultivate old memories or new ones

_____

Ideas to celebrate people or special occasions

_____

OCCASION #2:

_____

_____

Name of ritual and page number to use as a guide

_____

Ideas to create connections with the people in your life

_____

Ideas to cultivate old memories or new ones

_____

Ideas to celebrate people or special occasions

_____

_____

Personal Milestones

"Linda Ann Smith surprised my previous group of business compatriots with the 'What Would You Do if You Knew You Would Succeed?' ritual, complete with a gift certificate at a wonderful restaurant in New York City. The four of us participating in the ritual were all in fairly significant transitional stages. We finally made it to the restaurant with our package of ritual instructions and materials. The result was a profound opportunity for each of us to affirm the others for who we are in the world. It was one big warm fuzzy."

—Lisa Pike, Environmental Program Director,
Patagonia, Ventura, California

Graceful Grief

My women friends stood beside me as I buried my son. They walked beside me, pushed me, coaxed me and sometimes dragged me along the painful path of learning how to live again through the unspeakable grief of a mother's shattered life and heart. As my friends, they stood with me. As mothers, they felt my grief. As women, they helped ease my grief.

As the poet Adrienne Rich puts it, "The connections between and among women are the most transforming force on the planet." Without these women, I would not have been able to find a different way to live.

—Linda Ann Smith

Sharing Linda's loss dramatically changed my understanding of grief. What I came to understand is the uniqueness of the grieving process. When people grieve, they have thoughts, feelings and needs that are unique and that no one can fully comprehend.

Up until Linda lost her son, she functioned best in collaboration with others, so Linda's network of friends assumed she needed a collaborative approach to support her through her grief. With the best of intentions, we called a meeting of Linda's friends to design a support system with scheduled visits to take care of her. There was just one glitch: Linda wasn't inclined to have anyone around her. She needed to be alone. While this meant changing our plans, we did not abandon our intent. Throughout the many long months that Linda lived in what she later described as "a deep, dark hole," we created more subtle ways to support her, such as leaving voice messages to say we were thinking of her and dropping food off on her porch. When Linda eventually began poking her head out of the black hole, someone was always there to respond before she retreated. Eventually she stayed outside of the hole more than she was inside.

According to the actor Keanu Reeves, who has seen people he loves die young, "grief changes shape, but it never ends." Somewhere along this never ending journey, grieving people need and want help, because grief is just too overwhelming to survive alone. This ritual provides a flexible approach to supporting a friend on her unique journey through grief.

—Kelly Blair Roberts

Purpose

❖ Connect a network of friends to support a grieving friend.

❖ Capture significant events during the grieving friend's absence.

Preparation (Soon After the News of a Friend's Loss)

- ❖ Decide on a comfortable setting to hold a meeting.
- ❖ Contact the members of your friend's network and any family members who might want to be involved. Invite them to the meeting and let them know this is an opportunity to share ideas for supporting their friend through her grief.
- ❖ Buy some nice sheets of writing paper befitting the occasion. Title them: Significant Event in My Life You Would Want to Know About.

Presentation

- ❖ Give everyone an opportunity to share how this loss has affected them personally.
- ❖ Pass out the sheets of the titled writing paper for everyone to take away from the meeting to capture a significant occurrence over the next couple of months. These sheets will later be given to your grieving friend, when she is ready. In this way, she will have evidence of her presence in your lives—she will know that she was thought of—while she was grieving. For example, my work as a personal coach took off during the time Linda was grieving. I knew she would be interested in the details of my success with helping my clients make changes in their personal and professional lives.

❖ Generate a list of ideas for supporting your friend over the next few months.

❖ Designate someone to serve as a liaison between the group and your friend to communicate the kinds of support available. Let her know the group is standing by to support her. Identify which ideas appeal to her and if she has her own suggestions for how her friends can be of help.

❖ By phone or e-mail, compile and share the results of your meeting, including your own suggestions for how the group can activate their support. Encourage everyone to continue to exchange information during the first couple of months and to capture their significant event for sharing with your friend when she has begun to reconnect with friends and family.

❖ Because grief is a long and unique process, be prepared to adapt the group's efforts as your grieving friend's needs change over the months and years.

Other Ways to Go

❖ This ritual can be adapted to other circumstances, such as supporting a woman recovering from a serious illness or undergoing treatment for a chronic condition.

Future Pace

While traveling for business a few years ago, I was seated next to a friendly and curious man who was doing his best to start a conversation. Uncharacteristically, I am antisocial on airplanes, using the time to be quiet and read. However, this stranger was relentless about trying to drum up a conversation. I decided to use this opportunity to describe what I wanted to do in the future by talking about it in present tense.

This occurred about two years after I lost my son, Andrew, in a car crash. At an early age, Andrew was labeled "Attention Deficit Disorder," or A.D.D. I believe in alternative and homeopathic healing and chose this path to help Andrew. Along the way I found many remarkable resources to help A.D.D. children that profoundly changed both of our lives. So I described my life to the stranger on the plane as I envisioned it—helping people understand and work with Attention Deficit Disorder with a more holistic approach. The man was intrigued enough to ask for more information and give me his business card. I was inspired and energized by his interest. One result was www.andrewsinstitute.com, an on-line resource for A.D.H.D.

—Linda Ann Smith

Purpose

❖ Cultivate your desired future now.

Props

- ❖ Envelopes, paper and pens.
- ❖ Comfortable setting.

Presentation

- ❖ Supply everyone with an envelope to self-address.
- ❖ Place envelopes face down in the center. Each person in the group chooses someone else's envelope. If you want an element of surprise, do not reveal whose envelope you have selected.
- ❖ Take turns describing your desired future as though it were the present. This is an opportunity to relate your dreams, speaking in the present tense.
- ❖ Pay particular attention to, and even take notes on, the remarks made by the person whose envelope you selected. Listen not only to what she is saying but how she is saying it. Does her face light up? Does she get animated? Do the ideas keep coming?
- ❖ During, or as soon after the ritual as possible, write a letter to the person whose envelope you chose, offering affirmations about her desired future. Be creative. As you write, think what would be helpful to *you* to realize *your* dreams, and then extrapolate to what she might find helpful.
- ❖ Mail the letter and stand by, because no sooner will you send off the letter than you will receive one of your own.

Surgical Journey

A friend was scheduled to have surgery. In response to her request for friendly advice and support, I created a ritual to give her an opportunity to guide the experience rather than turning herself over to an impersonal medical system. The ritual also allowed her to be supported by her family in an active way. Here is her description of her surgical journey.

—Kelly Blair Roberts

Having never had surgery, I was apprehensive and tense. At first, preparing for the ritual added to my anxiety. I was worried about leading a ritual. I couldn't think of an image as the ritual required. But as I reviewed the steps of the ritual, I settled down. I became aware of the extended autumn weather and the beautiful colors of the changing leaves. That led to choosing a tree as my comforting image.

I invited my husband, son, daughter and several extended family members to join me. We gathered candles. I lit my candle, shared my image of a tree and the meaning it held for me. Trees are straight and strong but need tending and rejuvenating after the cold winter as they reawaken, grow anew, and blossom.

I asked my family (the youngest was nine) to hold this image and recall it during the day and time of my surgery. I watched each face in the circle as the candles were lit. Their faces glowed in the candlelight and reflected concentration, love and caring. I could feel the collective energy and it uplifted and calmed me.

On the day of my surgery, my sister-in-law called to wish me well. She described going on a walk that morning and noticing all the trees. On the second day after the operation, my son and daughter visited me in the hospital. They gave me a handmade card with a drawing of a sturdy, vibrant tree with a canopy of leaves going off the paper, into infinity. Their actions touched me deeply and I felt a greater bond with each of them.

I faced the surgery feeling mentally and physically ready. After the surgery, I regained my strength quickly. During my two-week and one-month post-op exams, my doctor called my recovery remarkable. While warned that depression was common, I didn't experience any. I know the ritual helped me to be optimistic and feel the support I needed for a successful surgical journey.

—Judy Wong

Purpose

❖ Cultivate a resourceful state of mind by providing loving support for a surgical experience.

53

Props

❖ A comforting image.

❖ Candles.

Preparation

❖ Spend time reflecting on all the positive elements you can associate with this experience and its desired outcome. For example, Garrison Keillor of *Prairie Home Companion* professed that recuperating from heart surgery was an opportunity to slow down and relax, time spent in a way he would never have experienced otherwise.

❖ Come up with an image that captures these positive elements in a compelling way. The image can be an object or symbol that represents some aspect of a surgical experience that is comforting and will lead to your recovery.

❖ Choose family members and friends you want to participate.

❖ Use candles with a color that resonates with your image.

Presentation

❖ Meet with your family members and friends at least a day before the surgery.

❖ Share your image with them and ask each to hold it in their mind's eye the day and time of surgery. Give each of them a candle to light and burn during the surgery while they hold your image and send you loving energy.

❖ Before you embark on your surgical journey, spend time with your own candle, visualizing your image and the wonderful people poised to support you.

❖ When you are recovered, share your experience and acknowledge your family and friends for their support.

Other Ways to Go

❖ Depending on how many participants you enlist, you could ask for their support on a staggered basis before, during and after the surgery. Or you can just trust that they will know when to connect with you.

❖ This ritual can also be used for other scary, stressful situations such as medical tests, important meetings, court dates—situations where the power of the mind and the benefit of optimism can make a difference.

Tend & Befriend

In an article in the April, 2006 issue of *Body+Soul* magazine, titled "Our Friends, Ourselves," the author establishes that having friends benefits both men and women. A study found that people with many personal friends had a sixty percent reduced likelihood of dying over the course of nine years. Researchers Shelley E. Taylor, Ph.D. and Laura Cousino Klein, Ph.D. discovered that women had an additional reaction they labeled "tend and befriend"—making friendship of paramount importance to women as they cope with stress.

This ritual was a collaborative brainstorm with my friend Katie. Her dear friend was going through severe challenges with recurring cancer, and Katie decided to bring all of her friends together in a show of emotional support and assistance.

—Linda Ann Smith

Purpose

❖ Cultivate support for a friend in need.

Props

❖ House plant or flower to plant.
❖ Potting containers or a garden.

Presentation

- ❖ Invite friends and family of the person being celebrated or supported who want to help.
- ❖ Ask everyone to bring a plant that symbolizes some aspect of the support recipient's personality—for example, a sunflower for a sunny disposition, lilacs for sweetness or a tiger lily because of her exotic nature.
- ❖ The plant represents new growth and well-being. Plant it in a garden in a place chosen by the friend in need, or plant the flower in containers in a sunny window inside the house.
- ❖ As each one plants her flower, ask her to share the symbolism of the flower.
- ❖ Close the ritual with everyone offering a gift such as bringing dinner over every Monday night or taking the friend grocery shopping one day a week for a month if she is unable to drive. The common denominator is to spend time with your friend.

The Third Act

In a three act play, the first act represents the introduction of characters and plot. Act two typically introduces conflict and provides for further development of plot and characters. It is not until act three that there is climax and resolution. If the play has been well set up, the third act can be very juicy.

In an interview promoting her autobiography, Jane Fonda talked about her life in three acts and what she is experiencing in her third act. "Early on in my third act I found my voice and, in the process, I have ended up alone but not really. You see, I'm with myself and this has enabled me to see feminism more clearly. It's hard to see clearly when you're a pretzel."

In a scene in the hit movie *Something's Gotta Give*, Frances McDormand, as sister to Diane Keaton's character, talks about how older women are getting better and more interesting while older men are dating younger women. As a single woman rapidly approaching sixty, I can tell you that no truer words have ever been spoken. Women who are interesting to begin with just get more so with or without men in their lives. The third act of a play—as well as your life—is the act that, according to Jane Fonda, "ties the other two acts together and makes the point."

See if these quotes resonate with you:

"I have become someone I would like to meet." Unknown.

"You would have to shoot me to put on stilettos." Unknown

"No is a complete sentence." Unknown

"Next time you are at the store, pick me up a jar of Neutrogena antiwrinkle cream." My mother, Cherrie Smith, around her 89th birthday

Louise Singleton, a former client of mine and a treasured friend, created a ritual for her 70th birthday. With her permission and editing, following is her "Third Act" ritual.

—Linda Ann Smith

Purpose

❖ Celebrate a birthday and cultivate a future of extraordinary possibilities.

Props

❖ A gathering of your girlfriends from as far back as you can reach. Louise had a girlfriend from elementary school attend.

❖ Flip chart paper and markers.

❖ A cozy hideaway cabin in the mountains or on a lake.

❖ Plenty of food, wine and chocolate.

Presentation

❖ Ask your friends to help you chart your life in decades using the flip chart paper and markers:
  ◆ Put in historical events and technological advances.
  ◆ Include wedding date(s), dates of your children's and grandchildren's births and other important dates.
  ◆ List your personal accomplishments and the life experiences that helped create the person you have become.
  ◆ List every place you have lived.
  ◆ Ask your friends to draw pictures and write affirmations along this chart of your life.
  ◆ Take this opportunity to really see yourself and who you are in the world. Accept the positive comments from your friends. Don't be shy about tooting your own horn.

❖ Take a break—that was intense. You laughed, you cried, your regrets still bring pain to your heart. Go for a hike or walk along the lake.

❖ Once you have returned from your break, ask your friends to help you map your Third Act. This is the act that will tie your first two acts together. This is the act in which you will make your point. You know you can create your life, drive your own change and choose how to react, act, feel and think. What talents, experiences and emotional strength can you draw upon from the first and second acts to assist you in achieving your Third Act?

❖ Then drink that wine, eat that chocolate and rejoice with your friends in a life well lived that holds great promise.

Footprints in the Sand

"Every beginning, after all, is nothing but a sequel, and the book of events is always open in the middle."

—Wislawa Szymborska

When a woman reaches her middle years, she may find herself feeling lost and unsure as her previous roles reach maturity. Questioning how to spend the *rest* of her life can be overwhelming.

Whether women experience a major midlife crisis or are challenged by minor disappointments, true friends are there for us, helping us find the gems of learning from minor disappointments and the strength to weather the major crises. This ritual is based on *affirmations and manifesting* for women open to receiving support for making change. Based upon our strengths and accomplishments, affirmations counter negative beliefs or doubts we may have about ourselves in trying times. Affirmations, like footprints in the sand, are evidence of our existence and the importance of the roles we play in the larger scheme of things.

Manifesting simply means being clear about what we want so it can come into our lives. Friends are just the ticket for extending affirmations and for providing support to move forward in our lives.

—Kelly Blair Roberts

Purpose

❖ Cultivate manifesting dreams.

Props

❖ A comfortable cozy setting.
❖ A container, small slips of paper and writing utensils.

Preparation

❖ Identify a focus person—someone who wants support to manifest her dreams.
❖ Meet with the focus person to schedule the ritual and identify who she wants to be present. Determine who will extend the invitations.
❖ Prepare a container to hold the written affirmations.
❖ Cut paper into small strips for recording her affirmations.

Presentation

❖ Assemble the group in a setting that is conducive to sharing.
❖ Explain the purpose and determine how people want to proceed with sharing their affirmations. Take turns stating a particular accomplishment or strength of the focus person, noting her own assessment of it and giving her the opportunity to comment. Then write it on a slip of paper and place in the container.

❖ Once the container is full and the stories are told, present the container to the focus person and ask her to share how she is feeling and how her perceptions of herself have been impacted.

Affirmation Protocol

❖ There are three simple guidelines for affirmations:
1) The focus person need not express thanks for each of the affirmations, although a singular closing expression of gratitude can be extended. We all deserve to be appreciated and need not feel indebted by affirmations.
2) The affirmations should be about the focus person rather than how the focus person does something for the supporter. For instance, "I appreciate you taking care of me," would be better framed as "I appreciate your capacity for nurturing others."
3) Be as specific as possible and provide examples— enjoy this opportunity to tell the stories of and about this unique human being.

About Manifesting

❖ The term manifesting may seem woo-woo, but all it really means is to reveal. In this context, manifesting results from having clarity about what you want, so it can show up. Having the support of others for getting what you want makes it all the more attainable.

Presentation

❖ The focus person identifies something she **wants** to show up in her life, preferably something that is attainable. Members of the group can be curious and help her to be really clear and specific about her request.

❖ Talk about what this will look, sound and feel like in the coming weeks and whether the focus person wants any support as it plays out.

Closure

❖ Take turns sharing any insights that occurred during the ritual.

❖ Congratulate the focus person on her resourcefulness and wish her the best for her personal journey.

On the Road Again

"Don't let a little dispute injure a great friendship."
—His Holiness the Dalai Lama

According to research from the Harvard Nurses' Health Study, having friends contributes to better overall physical functioning. When women are under stress, our bodies release a hormone that encourages us to band with other women for protection and support. Tending and befriending encourages the release of even more of the hormone, creating a calm state.

So what hormones are released when our friendships are under duress? If I'm in conflict with a friend, I am anything *but* calm. My entire body feels out of whack. Is it because we women are "tenders" that so many of us are uncomfortable with conflict?

Given my faith in the power of rituals, I decided to fashion a ritual for creatively engaging conflict based on Marshall B. Rosenberg's model called *Nonviolent Communication, A Language of Compassion*. Techniques from his model comprise this ritual for putting a friendship with a flat tire back on the road again.

—Kelly Blair Roberts

Purpose

❖ Cultivate an effective compassionate way to resolve conflicts and heal a troubled friendship.

Preparation

❖ Clarify the specifics of the conflict. What was said or done that caused you to feel what emotion?

❖ What need of yours got stepped on? We share basic human needs and the more directly we can communicate our needs, the easier it is for others to respond compassionately.

❖ What request might you pose to your friend that addresses your need—what specific action she could take?

❖ Call your friend to schedule a time and place to meet. Express your desire to clear something up with her. Share a few details about the issue if she wants a point of reference.

Presentation

❖ Begin the meeting by thanking your friend for agreeing to address this issue with you.

❖ Share the specifics of what occurred and the feelings you had as a result of what was said or done.

❖ Clarify what need of yours got stepped on and your request.

❖ Ask your friend to respond to what you have shared with her. Be curious about and open to her feelings and needs.

❖ Take the time to ensure you each understand the other's feelings and needs as you explore options for preventing this issue from occurring again between you.

❖ Once you both feel calm and clear about the conflict, take turns expressing what you value about each other and this friendship.

Other Ways to Go

❖ Do it in the moment! There is no reason to postpone addressing a conflict as it occurs—unless you are too upset in the moment to address it respectfully and in good faith or you need to clarify the specifics *before* talking it through. For example, if a friend says or does something that bothers you, express what you are feeling and what caused you to feel that way. Clarify your need in this circumstance. Ask your friend to respond to what you have shared. Explore together options for preventing this issue from occurring in the future.

Just for Fun

"I have slowly introduced my circle of friends to rituals. The rituals have to be fun-based, but I have noticed that the more I do the rituals with these resistant friends, the deeper they will go in sharing. There have also been a few miraculous outcomes such as the 'House Selling' ritual that is in the 'Woo-Woo' chapter."

Katie Coates, Regional Brand Manager
Phoenix, Arizona

I Always Wanted My Own Theme Song

"Without music, life is a journey through a desert."
—Pat Conroy

Every year at Christmas, I produce a Christmas card CD with a compilation of my favorite music. People who have received them over the years start calling me in August to confirm that their holidays will include another musical gift from me. Friends and clients have called me while they are listening to one of the CDs, just to tell me how much they enjoy the music. When the CD hits the mailboxes, amazing things sometimes happen: out of touch friends reconnect, acquaintances become friends and new business materializes.

Music has power! This ritual is based on the power of music and the belief that we all deserve a theme song. For you baseball fans, think about the theme songs played when a favorite player comes up to bat. What would your song be when you step up to bat one out of the park?
—Linda Ann Smith

Purpose

❖ Celebrate your very own theme song.

Props

❖ Chocolate and beverages of choice.

❖ A stack of favorite CDs (probably best to have them labeled with the participant's name) from each participant.

❖ A boom box—or hold the ritual in the room with the sound system.

❖ Paper and markers.

Preparation

❖ Invite a group of friends you believe will be inspired by having their own theme songs.

❖ Explain the ritual to invitees, asking them to be prepared with two or three song ideas and accompanying CDs, as well as favorite CDs to inspire further possibilities.

Presentation

❖ Present the reason for the ritual to the group: to find each person's theme song by either picking an appropriate song or writing one. Encourage each guest to choose a song that depicts what she needs to inspire and motivate her.

❖ Listen to possible theme songs together. Make a group effort to help each person choose a song. Before each person plays her possibilities, ask her to talk about what inspires her and what she wants her theme song to do. Allow time for the group to comment on the possibilities.

❖ When each person either writes or settles on her theme song, play each song and then ask the person to share why the song will help motivate and inspire her.

❖ Sing a verse of the song together to anchor it for the person.

❖ Ask someone to write a list of all the songs and then send copies of the list to everyone after the ritual.

❖ If you are feeling energetic, burn a CD of the all of the songs and give it to everyone who participated in this ritual.

Other Ways To Go

❖ Rent a karaoke machine and make it a production. Provide boas, tiaras and costume jewelry for an old-fashioned dress-up and sing your hearts out!

Ideas for Rituals for Just for Fun

OCCASION #1:

_____

Name of ritual and page number to use as a guide

_____

Ideas to create connections with the people in your life

_____

Ideas to cultivate old memories or new ones

_____

Ideas to celebrate people or special occasions

_____

OCCASION #2:

_____

Name of ritual and page number to use as a guide

_____

Ideas to create connections with the people in your life

_____

Ideas to cultivate old memories or new ones

_____

Ideas to celebrate people or special occasions

_____

Story Food

"Sometimes people need a story more than they need food."

—Jean Shinoda Bolen

One of our most fundamental needs as human beings is to tell our stories to people who will listen. The listeners perform the crucial role of "witnesses" to our lives and those who listen with their ears, hearts and souls will be rewarded by learning from, identifying with, and being inspired by the stories they hear.

Many books have been written about highly successful people and the attributes that make them successful or charismatic. On most of these lists is the ability to listen to someone as if she is the only person in the room and hers is the most important story in the world.

They know a secret: she is and it is . . . at least in that moment.

—Linda Ann Smith

Purpose

❖ Connect through the nurturing "food" of stories.

Props

❖ A bowl of beginning sentences for people to draw from or one beginning sentence for everyone.

Presentation

❖ Ask your guests to actively listen and avoid interruptions and/or ridicule.

❖ Take turns drawing an opening sentence or telling your story with the opening sentence provided.

❖ Examples of an opening sentence (an expanded version can be found on our *Dinner Talk Cards*© (available at www.PowerofRituals.com):

Have I every told you about the time I . . .

Something you don't know about me is . . .

My most embarrassing moment in school was . . .

I spent my formative years . . .

The event that helped make me who I am, was . . .

Other Ways to Go

❖ This ritual can be focused on someone's birthday, promotion, engagement or other life event. You can also use it to capture family stories on tape as a legacy for future generations.

Passion Soup Soiree

As a personal coach, I help my clients connect with their life passions. I see what a difference this can make to people seeking more fulfillment in their personal and professional lives as you will see in the testimonial written by my friend Kay Beaton. This ritual creates an opportunity for friends to cook up a special batch of soup made with ingredients symbolizing their passions.

—Kelly Blair Roberts

Photography was something I loved, but I chose a career as an engineer. Given the expense of acquiring a degree and the time it took to get established in the profession, I didn't think I could walk away from it to pursue photography. After my children were born, I quit working full-time to consult part-time. I still wasn't satisfied with my work life.

A turning point occurred when I broke my leg on the ski slopes and had some down time to heal. While my leg mended, my consulting work dried up and my interest in photography blossomed. Thanks to some coaching from my friend Kelly, I realized photography warranted more space in my life than as a hobby. I decided to take on any paying jobs I could get taking

*photos. I became an intern at the local newspaper and took
workshops to develop my skills.*

*Six years later, I am a professional photographer with an
impressive portfolio and a network of satisfied clients. I feel
blessed to be making a living doing something I love!*

—Kay Beaton

Purpose

❖ Celebrate the passion in your life.

Props

❖ Large kettle
❖ Soup broth
❖ Table settings
❖ Paper, pens, markers

Preparation

❖ Send out invitations asking that everyone bring an
   ingredient symbolizing what holds passion for them
   in their life. Side dishes and desserts are also welcome.
❖ Just before the guests arrive, put the soup broth in
   the kettle
❖ Set out bowls and utensils
❖ Set out the paper, pens and markers

Presentation

- ❖ As the guests arrive, arrange the ingredients in the kitchen.
- ❖ Once everyone has arrived, take turns with each guest presenting their passion and why they chose the ingredient to represent the passion.
- ❖ Do whatever is needed to combine the ingredients and put them in the kettle to cook.
- ❖ As a group, decide what seasonings to add to the soup
- ❖ While the soup simmers, relax and share your answers to these questions:
  - ◆ What is your greatest achievement and how did your passion help make it happen?
  - ◆ You are on the cover of a magazine. What magazine? Compose a headline that names your passion.
- ❖ When the soup is ready, set out the side dishes, serve the soup and enjoy the savory tastes of this group's passion soup.
- ❖ Over dessert, share your answers to this question:
  - ◆ How will your future be influenced by your passion?
  - ◆ Use paper, pens and markers to right affirmations to take with you.

Other Ways To Go

❖ Rather than the theme of passions, bring ingredients
that represent the person who influenced you most,
the love of your life, your life-long dream, your
favorite vacation.

❖ Instead of soup, bring ingredients for making a salad
or a pizza or an ice cream buffet.

Shoe Shopping Good . . . Or Shoe'n Tell

What woman hasn't rewarded herself, cured a bad mood, celebrated a triumph or replaced chocolate by buying a pair of new shoes? Carrie Bradshaw and her girlfriends on *Sex and the City* demonstrated, on a regular basis, how focusing on their shoes made them feel better. Celebrations around shoes are cropping up everywhere: the movie *In Her Shoes* is about sisters and shoes; QBC has a shoe sale to raise funds for breast cancer emceed by the *Desperate Housewives* stars. Shoe shopping with girlfriends is just about the best time you can possibly have.

A woman interviewed on an *Oprah* show told about purchasing a pair of Oprah's shoes at one of Oprah's clothing and shoe auctions to benefit charity. The woman took the shoes home and stood in Oprah's shoes for inspiration whenever she was depressed or blue. She reported that it helped her to "keep movin' on."

I wrote this ritual for my favorite clients, a group of women who work for a nonprofit organization and who happen to live in New York City (like Carrie Bradshaw and her friends). At the time I created this ritual, all of these women were in their thirties and all were stepping up their emotional and intellectual learning curves. As Christmas gifts, I purchased gift certificates for each of them at a New York shoe store, Otto Tootsi Plohound.

The gift certificates each came with a shoe metaphor as a directive. For Sarah, the executive director of the organization, the directive was to "buy a pair of shoes to kick butt in," because managing a nonprofit agency is a challenging job. For Lisa, the directive was to "buy a pair of shoes to strut your stuff in." She needed support to step out into her own strength. Annie was to "buy a pair of shoes to take a leap of faith in." And she did, signing up for graduate school, getting married and buying a house. For Polly, the directive was to "buy a pair of shoes to take the next step in." She was taking on more responsibility at the organization and building her knowledge and self-esteem.

Shoes are an exquisite metaphor for both the path in life you are walking and the attitude with which you walk. To quote Steven Tyler of Aerosmith, "There's nothing wrong with having bags under your eyes as long as you have shoes to match."

—Linda Ann Smith

Purpose

❖ Cultivate living your best life through the metaphors of shoes and, of course, getting a snappy new pair of shoes in the bargain.

Props

- ❖ Your favorite shoe store (in Denver it's Nordstrom's)
- ❖ Knowledge of what each girlfriend needs for support.
- ❖ Paper, pens, marker.

Preparation

- ❖ Invite shoe loving girlfriends.

Presentation

- ❖ Upon arrival at the shoe store, or even beforehand, tell the manager what you are doing. If you are all going to buy a pair of shoes at the conclusion of the ritual, the manager might very well run out to purchase a bottle of wine for you.
- ❖ Each shoe shopper writes on her card the specific reason for the shoes she is in search of. For example: take a leap of faith; kick butt; kick someone out the door; strut your stuff; step up to the plate; take the next big step on your life's journey; run towards something or someone; hit your stride. Have fun with the metaphors, applying them to wherever you want to go in life.
- ❖ Go get those shoes. Come back to the group with the shoes best depicting where you want your feet to take you, put the shoes on, and take turns talking about this important next step of your life.

❖ Ask for comments and support from the group, either written or verbal.

❖ Then buy those shoes and put your best foot forward, right out the door. A celebratory dinner following this ritual would put the spring in your step and be a good time to reflect on the next steps each woman will be taking in her new shoes.

To view this ritual in action filmed at the Nordstrom's shoe department in Denver, Colorado, go to www.PowerofRituals.com.

And the Question Is . . .

My good friend Sarah would end the yearly retreat her organization sponsored with a dinner at which someone would say, "Sarah, I believe we need a question." Whispering and behind-the-hand conferring would ensue with Sarah and the guests on either side of her. And "The Question" would spring forth. We eagerly anticipated this ritual as a moment when we could all have fun after putting in eighteen-hour days of meetings and events. This ritual was the impetus for our *DinnerTalk Cards*© (available at www.PowerofRituals.com.)

—Linda Ann Smith

Purpose

❖ Celebrate who you are and have fun with the answers.

Props

❖ Questions written on pieces of paper placed in a bowl or one question for each person to answer.

Presentation

❖ Either ask people to draw a question and answer the one they drew or post the question for everyone to answer.

❖ As in any group activity, ensure that people have a safe place to share. Setting guidelines regarding avoidance of ridicule or interruption helps create a positive experience.

❖ Examples of questions (see our *DinnerTalk Cards*© for more):

Who either changed your life or influenced your life in a big way—and how did he or she do it?

Who alive or dead would you like to spend an evening with and what would you talk about?

What was the best gift you have ever given and to whom?

Other Ways to Go

❖ Questions can be focused on a person you are honoring for one reason or another, on memories of past events or holidays, or on learning specific information about each other. Gather questions from other people. Start your own question collection.

Author! Author!

As there is a poem in everyone, there is a book in everyone. Whenever Kelly and I tell someone we are writing a book and what it is about, that person first places an order for at least five copies for gifts and her own use and then, inevitably, she tells us about the book she wants to write.

I gathered my suburban neighbors together one evening for dinner and in an attempt to put a little zing in the party, posed the question: "If you were to write a book, what would it be about?" There was an immediate enthusiastic response from everyone at the table. As each dinner guest shared the subject of his or her book—always a subject they had personal, sometimes dramatic, history with—the rest of us brainstormed possible book titles. These neighbors left with new information to help them build bridges of understanding.

—Linda Ann Smith

Purpose

❖ Cultivate and celebrate people's stories.

Props

❖ Dinner.

Preparation

❖ Invite friends and/or family to dinner, at home or at a restaurant.

Presentation

❖ This ritual can be spontaneous, posed as dinner table conversation that turns into group fun.

❖ Hearing the ideas of six to eight dinner guests could take some time. Pose the question early on: "If you were to write a book, what would the subject be?" That will allow everyone time to expound on their subject and time for the group effort of giving the book a title.

❖ If there is enough time, consider having members write book jacket blurbs they could imagine seeing on each book.

❖ As I was the host of the dinner in the story about this ritual, I wrote each person's book title on a piece of paper they took with them, as a memento of the night . . . and as inspiration. Who knows? I may soon be invited to a book signing.

❖ If your group is artistic, have materials available so people can design their own book covers.

Artists Unite!

Kelly and I could not write a book on rituals without one that focuses on art. In our history of friendship we have created and held art salons to celebrate birthdays, transitions and holidays. With the vast collection of art supplies in my garage/art studio, we have brought our friends together to create mirrors, clocks, collages—and, of course, there is always a ritual involved.

—Linda Ann Smith

Purpose

❖ Celebrate the artist within.

Props

❖ Art supplies.
❖ A place to work.

Preparation

❖ Advise your invited guests on the theme and project. List what you will have available (containers of water, paper towels, brushes, paints) and ask your guests to bring other supplies or bring a particular piece they want to include in their project.

❖ If you are celebrating something, decide on a theme and a type of art project, i.e., collage, watercolor, Christmas Cards, Thanksgiving centerpieces, etc.

Presentation

❖ Decide at which point in the process to introduce a ritual appropriate to the occasion. For instance, if you are adorning mirror frames in honor of someone's birthday, the ritual can be about what the guests "see" in the birthday person's future. Or if you are creating a collage, each person can talk about the metaphor of her life that came through in her collage.

❖ Remember that art is in the eye of the beholder. Turn off your preconceptions of what art should be and make it about what you like. It may be all about color, or it may have a personal message in what you draw or glue onto the piece.

Other Ways to Go

❖ Find a local art school and sign up for an art class together. Afterwards, take the art you made to a local coffee shop and share your experience as an artist.

Feed Your Inner Poet

Our friend, Kathryn Manning, is the inspiration for this ritual. Here, in her own words, is Kathyrn's story about finding her inner poet.

—Kelly Blair Roberts and Linda Ann Smith

When I was given a writing class for my birthday ten years ago, I was excited and terrified, all at the same time.

'What if I can't write, anymore?' I asked my husband Duane.

'Of course, you can still write! It isn't so much about what you do as who you are,' he replied.

To my delight, I discovered I still loved writing and was amazed how the words flowed when the instructor detailed a writing exercise and shouted, "Go!"

*One October morning two years ago, I went to my part-time job selling Italian ceramics to discover I no longer **had** that job. I left the store, shocked and dejected, mumbling, "It's all good, it's all good," and stopped at the drug store on my way home. I walked the Halloween aisle filled with black capes and witches' hats, gray stringy wigs and scary masks. And then I saw them: rack upon rack of brightly-colored feather boas. Just like the brightly colored Italian ceramics!*

I bought four boas, each a different color, and drove to another drug store where I bought four more boas in four more colors. I drove home and told Duane, "I don't have a job, any-more! But look at these great feather boas!" A conversation ensued about life, writing, feather boas—and the idea for M&M Boetry© emerged.

*Remembering my doubt in my ability to write and know-ing that many of my friends don't believe in their own ability to create, I decided to show them they could at a holiday gath-ering with feather boas and M&M's®. I am now the co-author of **Boetry Collections, Writing Your Soul's Poem** and plan a reunion Boetry© party for 2008.*

—Kathryn Manning

Purpose

❖ Cultivate your inner poet.

Preparation

❖ Invite six women to your Boetry© party. (More is okay but six keeps the gathering to three hours.) The gathering can be an evening of appetizers, a Saturday lunch or a Sunday brunch.

❖ Purchase six small bags of M&M's® and create your list of 15-20 color-words for the six colors of M&M's®: brown, red, blue, yellow, green and orange. For example, brown words might be *Earth,* Cave, *Grandmother, Wood* and *Antique.* Blue words

could include *Light*, *River* and *Winter*. Make six
columns of words, each headed with the word
of the color they represent. Make a copy for
each guest.

❖ Provide materials for writing: the color-word list
(rolled and tied with a ribbon), bag of M&M's®,
pen, pencil, and writing pad or journal that they can
take home with them.

❖ Purchase various colors of feather boas and lay them
out for your guests to choose. You can even hang
them on a silk ficus plant and call it the Boa Tree!

❖ Create an atmosphere of tranquility and beauty in
which the women feel safe and free to let their
feelings surface. Be creative and colorful in setting
your table.

❖ A theme will emerge. It may be the same for all
women or unique to each woman. There's no need to
push or pull; what needs to be expressed will be
expressed.

Presentation

❖ Greet each guest as she arrives and ask her to choose
a feather boa to wear. Offer her food and drink,
introduce her to other guests, and show her where
to sit.

❖ Refrain from explaining what will happen. Just allow
the women to talk and share for about an hour.

❖ When the moment presents itself, share the Boetry© concept of writing a poem. Assure your guests: that the poem is within them and will present itself; that there is no good or bad poem; that there are no rules regarding rhyme or meter. Ask your guests to empty their bags of M&M's® onto the table, separate the colors into six piles, and then open the color-word list.

❖ Tell your guests they will have about thirty minutes to choose (and write down) words according to the colors of their M&M's® and write their poem. For example, if they have three brown M&M's®, they will write down three brown words, five red words if they have five red M&M's®, and so on. Suggest that it is the poem within them choosing the words; therefore, it is important to go with the words that speak to them.

❖ Each guest should begin writing her poem by simply looking at their words and going with whatever thought comes to her first. Stress that it is important to not question the direction or destination of the poem. The women are not the poems, but the instruments through which the poems emerges. (Variations of a word are okay, i.e. *Joy* can become *Joyful*. If they have a couple of words left over that just don't fit in, it's okay to omit them. If someone senses two poems emerging rather than one, that's okay, too!)

Other Ways to Go

❖ Have a Boetry© party annually, inviting six different women or one additional new woman, or perhaps two from a previous party and four new women. It's up to you!

❖ Generate anticipation by having the Boetry© party at the same time every year. If you decorate for Christmas, this is a great time to *feed your inner poet* as the lights and color spark creativity!

❖ Suggest wearing a turtleneck or collar that can be turned up so the feather boa isn't against the skin (they can be a bit scratchy!)

❖ Try Boetry© with couples! Men are wonderful poets!!

Boetry© Poem Example

BREATHE

"Birth is the struggle, the stormy, fiery sunrise dance.
Embrace the fall; seize the grace
And the lone volcano night becomes
the soft moon freedom of life.
Step to the window of joy into the lush, bold forest
And make a friend with life.
Breathe.
You will return to the island of clouds when it is time."
—Kathryn Manning

Telling Stories

"The stories people tell have a way of taking care of them. If stories come to you, care for them. And learn to give them away where they are needed. Sometimes a person needs a story more than food to stay alive."

—*Crossing to Avalon,* **Jean Shinoda Bolen, MD**

Everyone Has a Story

(Thanks to *The Oprah Winfrey Show*)
Inspiration and ideas for rituals are everywhere. *The Oprah Winfrey Show* is a treasure chest of ideas. To demonstrate the indisputable fact that "everyone has a story," a guest on one of her shows threw darts at a seating chart of her audience. Everyone occupying a seat that drew a dart had a remarkable story.

People are feeling disconnected these days. They are hungry to tell their stories and be heard. The hearing part is the challenge. Taking the time to hear someone's story is an act of great unselfishness—and one that is often a source of inspiration and knowledge for the listener, as well.

I work and live alone in my house, with hours spent on the computer or telephone, so telephone chatting is not high on my list of ways to connect. Connecting with my friends is increasingly difficult with Denver's population growth causing wearying traffic jams and highway angst. I find that when I do connect with a friend, I tend to "spill" everything I have been doing, thinking, wanting. I have to consciously remember to hear *their* story when I am so intent on someone hearing *mine*.

I usually practice this ritual when I travel so I don't feel as alone. If anyone—at any time or any place—even looks at me sideways, I consciously connect with them. Often, I don't even have to ask the person to tell me their story. Once I have connected with someone, the story just seems to come naturally.

When we finally part to board planes, I always hear, "Thank you."

Although I usually do this ritual one-on-one, involving a group of family or friends is equally powerful since there is more than one person hearing and reacting to one's story.

—Linda Ann Smith

Purpose

❖ Cultivate deeper understanding and knowledge in your relationships.

Props

❖ Tape recorder and a tape for each friend.

Presentation

❖ Make the ritual more useful to the speaker by taping the story. Self-consciousness disappears surprisingly quickly, and the person who has been talking is left with a record of what she may consider the most important events of her life. The recording can be a continuing source of self-revelation for the storyteller.

❖ Ask the question: "What is your story?"
❖ You can also ask the question with a focus:
    What is your story about sports in high school?
    What is your story about dating in college?
    What is your story about your "grand passion?"
    What is your story about your first job?
    What is your story about something you did that
       took your breath away?
❖ After you ask the question, listen with your whole being.
❖ Finally, hand each friend her labeled recording as she leaves.

"I used to hide in the bathroom when a ritual was announced. Now my advice to all men is to stay out of the bathroom because you will lose out on a lot of good material. Once you get past the shock, and if people participate, it can turn out to be an experience in which you get understanding and information—all that warm fuzzy stuff. Plus it's a good way for men to win points with women."
—**Stephen Smith, Entrepreneur, Denver, Colorado**

Metaphor Magic

To break the monotony of a long drive across Kansas, I created the Kansas Wheat Field Ritual.

"What," I asked my passengers, "about your life is like a Kansas wheat field?"

I was surprised by the enthusiasm of my captive audience. The responses were eloquent, heartfelt and enlightening. My Aunt Frances answered that the Kansas wheat field is a metaphor for her family and their family. We each talked in more detail about our answers and arrived at our destination with a deeper understanding and connection.

Metaphors, which find the similarities between unlike objects or ideas, provide a creative way to express emotions, ideas, a vision, or desire. Most people use metaphors regularly without realizing it when they talk about being hungry as a bear or someone who is pretty as a picture.

To help you tap your own ideas for concocting metaphors, we offer these examples as *food for thought* for *fanning the flames* to *get your feet wet* and *give free rein* to your imagination.

—Linda Ann Smith and Kelly Blair Roberts

Purpose

❖ Connect to your relationships through personal insights with a metaphorical question as the tool.

Props

❖ Settings conducive to sharing, such as sitting around a table, riding in a car, or taking a walk. This ritual doesn't need to be official. Do it spontaneously.

Presentation

❖ Conjure up and agree on a metaphorical question to pose to the group. Here are a few examples:

What part of the pizza are you and why?

What aspects of your life is like a river?

If you were a piece of sport equipment what would you be and why?

❖ Take turns sharing. Be curious. Ask deeper questions of the person who is talking.

Voices of Experience

❖ "I laughed when I read this ritual because it was so familiar. I have a group of friends from college and we have been doing this for years. I can tell you in grand detail what part of a dinner all these people are—for instance, I've always been happy to be pumpkin pie with whipped cream."

—Lisa Ray Turner aka Pink Diva

❖ On a Habitat for Humanity trip to Hungary, I
proposed the Blue Danube Ritual. The question to
the group was, "What element of the Blue Danube
does each team member represent?" After twelve
days of working and playing together, we knew each
other very well and could easily associate everyone
with a unique element. Alex was a bubbling creek,
because of his spontaneous quips of humor, while
Hal was the undercurrent, because of his strong
support of the team.

—Linda Smith

"Rituals come in handy when it comes to my work. As a mediator, I find it very useful to take a moment before the disputants arrive to sit and close my eyes. I expand an image of a balloon of love and light until it fills every single crack and crevice of the room. It seems to help the disputants stay calm and more open to possibilities and it helps me protect my core energy."

—Kristin Thompson, Mediator

Write 'N Hike

I created this ritual to combine hiking with creative writing to celebrate a friend's birthday. As my group of friends gets older, having the same old birthday party is just not compelling. This ritual connected us all to the birthday girl, cultivated memories and understanding and celebrated her birthday in a unique and joyful way.

—Linda Ann Smith

Purpose

❖ Celebrate a special event that will connect the participants and cultivate memories.

Props

❖ Pens and paper.
❖ A timer.
❖ Hiking gear and supplies (water, food, chocolate, etc.).

Preparation

❖ Choose an event to celebrate (such as a birthday or upcoming wedding) or find an excuse to spend time with girlfriends and invite a group of gal-pals.

Presentation

- ❖ Identify a focus for the creative writing.
- ❖ Design questions or unfinished sentences to use as prompts, ideas to write about, or outlandish subjects to explore, such as "What would I name myself and why?" There is no right or wrong to this—just be creative with ways to fuel the writing.
- ❖ Start hiking with your friends.
- ❖ Take turns picking spots to stop and write. Look for breathtaking views, rocks and logs to sit on and/or streams to sit by.
- ❖ Agree on the prompt or subject, set the timer for ten minutes and start writing. At the sound of the timer, take another minute to complete the writing.
- ❖ Take turns reading what you wrote.
- ❖ Be supportive of both the laughter and tears that can emerge.
- ❖ Consume and savor a chunk of chocolate. Start hiking again, stopping further down the trail to write again.
- ❖ Repeat until everyone has chosen a spot, or all the chocolate has been gobbled up.
- ❖ Complete the ritual by sharing favorite moments, insights or writing.

Examples of Prompts

- ❖ The last time I saw . . .
- ❖ I am most proud of . . .
- ❖ What would my own personal theme song be and why?
- ❖ I have always wanted to tell you . . .
- ❖ My wildest dream is to . . .

Other Ways to Go

- ❖ Potluck Prompts: Each time you stop to write, a prompt or subject can be contributed by a different person.
- ❖ Particular Person Prompts: If the write 'n hike is taking place because of a birthday or special occasion, the birthday girl can think up the prompts. For example, the birthday girl in this ritual story asked her friends to capture a fond memory involving her. Many of us chose to share our first memory of meeting her. Not only did this connect each of us to the birthday girl but also created a sense of connection with each other.

"(Author) Linda Ann Smith and I met 20 years ago as neighbors and single mothers. We connected quickly and deeply, and created many extraordinary memories with each other and with our sons.

I have always appreciated Linda's talent for creating special moments in her relationships with others, including my family and her son Andrew. Many of those special moments were a result of an inspirational ritual created by Linda, motivating those around her to search for new and fun ways to deepen the connection between themselves and loved ones.

Linda has touched me with unusual ways to speak from the heart and make those special connections that stay with us for a lifetime. The rituals encourages us to push through our 'way too comfortable' communication boundaries to a new level of connection, You will enjoy her talent of improving relationships with rituals in a fun and creative way."

—Dana Smith, Financial Manager Consultant

The Empty Chair

Sometimes a ritual develops by accident. One night during a Habitat for Humanity trip to Budapest, our team of seven was seated at a table with eight chairs. Our team leader looked at the chair and remarked that we were missing a person—and a ritual was born. Who were we missing? As those at the table talked about who they would put in the chair and why, this trip to build walls became a chance to build friendships.

—Linda Ann Smith

Purpose

❖ Cultivate sharing unknown and surprising aspects of people's lives.

Props

❖ A table with a chair for everyone and one extra chair.

Presentation

❖ Conduct the ritual at any time during the meal. When the participants are not longtime friends, doing it at the beginning of the meal works particularly well, serving as an icebreaker. Whether new friends or long term ones, what everyone learns can spark an ongoing conversation and ongoing connections.

❖ Choose a theme or a category of people to fill the chair: an absent family member, ancestor, historical figure, movie star, friend, etc.

❖ Ask each person at the table to choose who they would invite to sit in the chair.

❖ Ask each person to explain their choice. What would you ask the person if s/he was seated with the group? Why is s/he important to you? What would you want the person in the chair to know about you?

Voice of Experience

❖ I put my father in the chair. The most cherished times I have spent with my dad have been working with him in his carpentry shop after he retired from his demanding Air Force career. We moved to a greater appreciation of each other by building everything from retaining walls to furniture together.

—Linda Ann Smith

The Name Game

Do you love or hate your name? Do you think you would look different or act different if you had a different name? Do you believe you would have a different life with a different name? Well, I do. With a stunning lack of imagination my parents gave me a profoundly simple name. Over the years I have picked it apart in a vain attempt to give it some pizzazz. For many years I told everyone that Linda means "pretty" in Spanish. I have yearned for a name that would celebrate my Italian heritage. If you knew me you would definitely see me as a "Lucia."

Ask someone the origin or family history of their name, and then stand back. Your name is the first thing you hear from your parents and you keep on hearing it, not only from them, but from every person you know—for the rest of your life. Over a lifetime, your name is spoken to you in sounds of endearment, anger, commands, disappointment. Your name is your most intimate possession, intertwined with and integrated into your personal identity. It is also the basis of a ritual that can reveal things about you to your closest friends they never would have imagined and things about them that will give you new understanding.

—Linda Smith

Purpose

❖ Cultivate interesting information about a person through their name.

Presentation

❖ Ask the following questions and be prepared to take notes:

Tell me about your name.

If you could change you name, what would it be and why?

What do you like about your name?

What Would You Do
If You Knew You Would Succeed?

In 1996, we celebrated our family Christmas at my brother, Larry's home in Phoenix. The holiday included a dinner at an elegant restaurant to celebrate December birthdays and anniversaries. I volunteered to create a ritual and, as usual, my family did a collective cringe—except for my son Andrew. That boy was always ready for a ritual.

I had no idea what kind of ritual I would create, but trusted one would evolve prior to the evening of the dinner. Then, when Andrew and I were breezing through Barnes and Noble on the day of the dinner, my eyes locked onto a rack of postcards. I came to a screeching halt at the rack, with Andrew literally running right into me. As I stared at the postcards, the idea for the ritual began to form. I pulled postcards off of the rack with pictures that reminded me of each member of my family. For instance, the card I chose for my brother Larry featured a man wrapped in black, standing in a meditative pose on a tree branch. Since Larry possesses an interesting mixture of unconventional (up a tree, one might say) and Zen-like qualities, the card seemed to suit him perfectly. Andrew helped me choose a unique card for each family member.

At dinner, each person was presented with the postcard selected for them and instructed to write on its left side what they would do if they knew they would succeed. The cards were passed around the table for the other members of the family to write, on the right hand side, why they knew that person would succeed at what s/he wanted. We then took turns verbally affirming the person on why they would succeed.

Members of my family were truly surprised at what others wanted to do, and truly touched when they found out how others in the family felt about them. We caused quite a stir in the restaurant. I discovered later that some of my family members kept their postcards in special places so they could refer to them often, as touchstones to help them through difficult times or decisions. My card pronounced that I would be a "best selling author." My son Andrew's affirmation was that I would succeed because I was "very creative." He underlined creative twice.

The memory of this ritual is bitter-sweet for my family. This was the last Christmas we had with my son Andrew. We lost Andrew in a car crash on February 12, 1997. I found his postcard in his school assignment calendar.

—Linda Ann Smith

Purpose

❖ Celebrate the uniqueness in each person.

Props

❖ One postcard for each person or a blank card of any kind.

❖ Pens.

Presentation

❖ Each person answers the following question on the left side of her postcard: What would you do if you knew you would succeed?

❖ Someone takes the lead and gathers the cards.

❖ The leader chooses a card and asks the person to share what she wrote on the card in answer to the question posed.

❖ That card is then passed along to the others at the table. One at a time, each person offers a supportive comment and writes it on the card, then passes the card on to the next person until everyone at the table has provided support, both verbally and in writing.

❖ Repeat the process for each person at the table.

Other Ways to Go

❖ After each participant has written her answer to the question on her card, all of the cards are passed around at once for supportive notes, with each person writing a supportive comment on the cards of all the other women. When finished, each woman takes a turn reading aloud the supportive comments written for her.

Ideas for Rituals for Telling Stories

OCCASION #1:

_____

_____
Name of ritual and page number to use as a guide
_____

_____
Ideas to create connections with the people in your life
_____

_____
Ideas to cultivate old memories or new ones
_____

_____
Ideas to celebrate people or special occasions
_____

_____

OCCASION #2:

_____

_____
Name of ritual and page number to use as a guide
_____

_____
Ideas to create connections with the people in your life
_____

_____
Ideas to cultivate old memories or new ones
_____

_____
Ideas to celebrate people or special occasions
_____

_____

Woo-Woo

"Rituals, the sacred acts and languages that symbolize our life cycles, are vital to bridging the gaps between our psyches, emotions, spirituality, and experiences. Rituals establish our images of self and identify us in the human community. Rituals of day-to-day living, special occurrences, and intimacy inform our relationships and our sacred spaces. Rituals, essentially, are testimonials to our beliefs about our loved ones, ourselves, our deities, and our world."

The Reverend Dr. Marjorie Williams-Cooper,
Healer, Artist & Educator, Denver, Colorado

Answers from Our Ancestors

Role models can motivate and inspire you to overcome hardships, make difficult decisions and stand as your own advocate. Stories abound in my family about their survival in a world fraught with hardships: World War I, World War II, the Korean War, the Great Drought and men coming home from war to an economically depressed country. Throughout American history, half of the immigrants flooding to this land of opportunity have been women. They have often fled lives of despair, coming to America to begin again. My Italian grandmother was one such woman travelling across a vast ocean with all of her belongings in a small trunk to start a new life in a country where she did not even speak the language. I can't even muster up enough hutzpah to move across town!

Our female ancestors had backbones of steel, eyes filled with determination and spirits that breathed belief in themselves and their capabilities. Such character and grit is rarely seen in this age of excess and entitlement.

Do you ever catch yourself whining about your life, what you don't have, and the innumerable silly annoyances that constitute too much of your time? I offer this ritual to connect into the wisdom, strength and sacrifices of your female ancestors to use as inspiration for making changes in your life and igniting a sense of gratitude each day. It will also remind you that these worthy female ancestors contributed to the genetic makeup that is *you*.

—Linda Ann Smith

Purpose

❖ Connect to your ancestral strength to change your life.

Props

❖ Photos and stories of female relatives the participants admire.
❖ A table and the means for propping up photos for display.
❖ 3x5 cards, pens and markers.
❖ An easel with a flip chart and markers.

Presentation

❖ Ask each woman to present the photo of her ancestor and prop it up on the table so everyone can picture the woman as her story is told.
❖ Ask someone in the group to capture the adjectives used to describe the ancestors on the flip chart.
❖ Following the stories, review the adjectives and discuss: how you currently use the strengths

and wisdom of your female ancestors in your life and how you can better tap into them to effect desired changes in your life; how the lessons you have learned from your ancestors' lives have helped you; and will continue to help you, as you make your own journey through life; the aspects of your life for which you have a better sense of gratitude thanks to your understanding of your ancestors' lives, and; how you plan to tap into the richness of your genetic heritage.

❖ Invite each woman to write one or two adjectives on a 3x5 card to pull out when in a whining or complaining frame of mind.

What is your heritage? Italian? Dutch? Vietnamese? No matter what country you claim as your roots, no matter how distant, you can discover pearls of wisdom, extraordinary life stories and lessons by interviewing an older relative. Here are a few things to remember when you prepare for your interview.

Bring a tape recorder or video camera to the interview and paper and pens to capture the treasure chest of information.

Prepare a list of questions for the interview and provide the list to your interviewee prior to the interview. Schedule a time for the interview.

Ask questions that will encourage your subject to talk and expand on the subject. Keep your own comments and questions brief and to the point.

Sample Questions:
1. Basic historical information: Name, age, place of birth, parents names.
2. What is the meaning behind your name? Were you named after a relative and why?
3. Where were your parents born?
4. How did your parents meet?
5. What did your parents do for a living?
6. What did you do for a living?
7. What ritual was passed down from family members that you still prepare for your family?

Websites for further searches:
www.familysearch.org
www.genaology.com
www.ancestorhunt.com
www.rootsweb.com
To start a family website: www.myfamily.com

Circle the Wisdom

"The circle is an ancient and universal symbol of unity and wholeness. For many millennia human beings have met in tribal or village circles to tell stories, provide mutual support, and arrive at an understanding of the common good."
—Excerpted from *Wisdom Circles, A Guide to Self-Discovery and Community Building in Small Groups*, by Cindy Spring, Charles Garfield, and Sedonia Cahill

I have countless memories of circular experiences: playing round robin games as a kid; sitting around a campfire; my friends encircling a Victorian house on a summer evening in Kansas to launch a housewarming party; standing with my girlfriends on a snowy mountain in Colorado, gazing at the circle made by our snowshoes.

This ritual provides a structure for women to tap the power of circles for conducting dialogues, sharing wisdom, and building community. Elements of this approach to meeting in circles have been drawn from the book *Wisdom Circles, A Guide to Self-Discovery and Community Building in Small Groups* by Charles Garfield, Cindy Spring, and Sedonia Cahill.

Try this approach at your next meeting. I guarantee it will enhance the intimacy and depth of your conversations.
—Kelly Blair Roberts

Purpose

❖ Connecting, telling stories and building community.

Props

❖ A comfortable setting in which the participants can sit in a circle.

❖ A talking stick (an object that is passed around to be held as the participants are speaking).

❖ Objects to mark the center of the circle such as a cloth, candles and items that are symbolic to the purpose of the group.

Preparation

❖ Invite a group of women connected by some common purpose.

❖ Based upon the interests of the group, choose a topic to pose in the form of a question. A group may choose an issue specific to its collective needs or there may be topics arising from the needs of one or more individuals.

❖ Gather the objects that will mark the center of the circle.

❖ Arrange for a meeting place.

❖ Arrive early to mark the center of the circle and arrange the seating in a circle.

Presentation

❖ Open the ritual with something simple to get everyone focused such as reading a poem, sharing a few minutes of quiet or listening to a piece of music. Light the candles in the center of the circle and explain the choice of objects. Present the talking stick.

Round I

❖ Pose the question. (See the "Sample Questions" section for ideas.)

❖ Take turns responding to the question with each speaker holding the talking stick and sharing without interruption.

❖ Listening is the primary activity and silence is important throughout this process. That is, the only person talking should be the woman holding the talking stick. Silence should be maintained as the talking stick is being replaced in the center of the circle and chosen by another speaker. This contrasts sharply to our normal patterns of cross-talk.

❖ Keep rotating until no one has anything else to say and there is a sense of completion.

Round II

❖ Pose this question: What is the collective wisdom our dialogue has revealed?

❖ As before, take turns responding with the talking stick until there is a sense of completion.

Round III

❖ Pose this question and take turns responding: What should we do with this? (Are there actions to be taken or information to be compiled and shared?)
❖ Close the ritual by summarizing the outcomes of the three rounds of dialogue. Thank everyone for their participation and blow out the candles.

About the Talking Stick

❖ The talking stick or object stays within the center of the circle. Before speaking, each person reaches for the talking stick and replaces it when she is finished speaking.
❖ The purpose of the talking stick is to give the person holding it the right to speak without interruption. Use of the talking stick helps groups pace the dialogue, empowering individuals to speak and focusing the rest of the group on listening.
❖ Any object can be used: an actual stick, a rock, a seashell or something that represents what the group stands for.

Framing the Questions

❖ Choose questions that require thinking rather than *yes* or *no* responses.

❖ Choose questions that will cause the participants to reflect on personal experience or share a story.

Sample Questions

❖ What can we learn from our own and each other's experiences?

❖ What is our vision?

❖ If you could change one thing about the world, what would it be?

Other Ways to Go

❖ This process works best for small groups to ensure everyone has a chance to share. If there are more than six participants, consider breaking into two groups. Use the closing to share the outcomes of both groups.

❖ For special occasions such as birthdays and anniversaries, have the celebrants pick a topic to explore at their event with friends and family.

Ideas for Woo-Woo Rituals

OCCASION #1:

_____

Name of ritual and page number to use as a guide
_____

Ideas to create connections with the people in your life
_____

Ideas to cultivate old memories or new ones
_____

Ideas to celebrate people or special occasions
_____
_____

OCCASION #2:

_____

Name of ritual and page number to use as a guide
_____

Ideas to create connections with the people in your life
_____

Ideas to cultivate old memories or new ones
_____

Ideas to celebrate people or special occasions
_____
_____

New Home Wishes

The following ritual was designed as a family blessing for my brother Larry and sister-in-law Gloria's new home in Phoenix Arizona. We gathered in their new home to celebrate Christmas and I arrived with this ritual. The stones in this ritual were based on honoring the southwest Native American culture in the area.

—Linda Ann Smith

Purpose

❖ Celebrate the hopes and dreams a new home brings.

Props

❖ Stones and wishes written on cards, brought by the participants.

Preparation

❖ Suggest the ritual to a friend or family member who has moved into a new home or take advantage of a gathering already scheduled.
❖ Ask those who will be attending to bring stones or wishes written on cards.

Presentation

- ❖ Gather in the kitchen—as the symbol of the heart of the home—with the stones and cards.
- ❖ The home owners share:
  - ◆ Their wishes for their new home.
  - ◆ Anticipation of things to come in this new home.
  - ◆ Experiences and memories from their last home they want to bring into this home.
- ❖ Family and friends share their own stories about the new homes they have moved into and the homes left behind.
- ❖ Guests take turns reading blessings or wishes for the new home.
  - ◆ The group moves out to the yard and each person places her stone in the yard or garden.

Other Ways to Go

- ❖ Plant a tree as a group.
- ❖ Guests bring a perennial flower to plant that symbolizes what they wish for the family, e.g. daisies for happiness or tulips for joyful surprises.
- ❖ Bring a silk flower with your wish written on a small card and tied to the flower. As you share your wish, place the flower in a vase. The vase becomes a constant reminder of the good wishes bestowed on the owners of the home.

Critical Care

I work as a long-term care ombudsman advocating for residents in nursing homes and assisted living residences. I came to this work because of my experiences home hospicing my father and then three years later my mother. End-of-life circumstances bring out the best and worst in people. As a family, we were fortunate to experience the best in each of us and our parents as they died.

This ritual is based on the premise that people facing end-of-life and major medical challenges can't get enough love and support—before, during and after.

Recently, one of my dearest girlfriends contracted meningitis and almost died. As she lay in intensive care for a week, I found myself focusing on how much I would miss her if she didn't recover. Feeling that this focus was helping neither of us, I decided to write my friend a letter she could read upon her recovery. Instead of worrying about her, I spent time recalling fond memories the two of us share and articulating what I hold most dear about her. When word finally came that she was in the clear, I breathed a sigh of relief and relished the experience of writing a letter in which I was connecting with her aliveness rather than her illness. I plan to share the letter on her next birthday, which will be an exceptional one—after all, she lived to see it.

—Kelly Blair Roberts

Purpose

❖ Cultivate values, beliefs, life lessons, hope, love and forgiveness in a letter to be shared.

Preparation

❖ Your motivation to write the letter will be unique to each relationship. Determine when and with whom the sending of a love letter seems appropriate to you. Is your girlfriend getting married? Divorced? Having a baby? Sending a kid off to college? Changing careers? Losing a parent? And so on. Any significant life passage or important occasion lends itself to receiving a letter of values.

❖ Pick a theme for the letter. Here are some possibilities:

Themes from the Past:

- ◆ Meaningful memories and stories.
- ◆ Lessons learned.
- ◆ Regrets.

Themes from the Present:

- ◆ Values and beliefs.
- ◆ Expressions of love and gratitude.
- ◆ Apologies.

Themes for the Future:

- ◆ Blessings, dreams and hopes.
- ◆ Advice and guidance.
- ◆ Requests.

Presentation

❖ Create an outline with the themes you want to address.

❖ Just write! Don't edit your thoughts.

❖ Arrange what you have written.

❖ Add an opening paragraph and a conclusion.

❖ Set the document aside for several days, or even weeks, and then review and edit it.

❖ Send the letter or deliver it in person. Ask your recipient if the two of you can have a conversation when she has had time to read and process it. Talk about what it meant to write the letter and what it meant to your girlfriend to receive the letter.

Other Ways to Go

❖ Keep a journal with entries noting when a friend does or says something that touches you or with notes on something you think bears honoring about her. Then share your thoughts on her birthday.

❖ Write a letter to a girlfriend facing a medical or surgical challenge.

❖ Write a letter to a girlfriend who may have hurt you in some way, thanking her for the unexpected lessons that resulted from the conflict and forgiving her.

"My daughter and I take an annual trip together as the first part of our ritual. A few years ago, I asked Linda for some ideas on how to deepen and enrich our experience together on these trips. After some brainstorming with her, I came up with the idea of bringing a travel journal with us on each of the trips and taking turns writing in the journal. We have such a good time re-reading what we wrote on the previous trips. We never leave the journal behind. It's the first thing in the suitcase."

**—Linda Stevens, Fourth Grade Teacher,
Centennial, Colorado**

Pearls of Wisdom

> "Share your knowledge. It's a way to achieve immortality."
> —His Holiness the Dalai Lama

I have been blessed with the presence of many mentors in my life, women whose willingness to share their experiences and expertise made it possible for me to succeed. This ritual is dedicated to the wisdom so many women have and are willing to share with others. It is a simple structure for collecting the individual wisdom of professionally-affiliated women.

> —Kelly Blair Roberts

Purpose

❖ Celebrate, share and honor the wisdom of professional women.

Props

❖ A professional gathering or event.
❖ Written instructions and index cards.

Preparation

❖ Compose a simple explanation and instructions (see sample below).

❖ Duplicate the explanation and instructions on slips of paper for distributing, along with an index card, to the participants.

Sample Instructions

Please take a few minutes to answer the following question on the index card and be sure to sign your name. Question: *If you had to pick one quality for all (name the profession) to have, what would it be and why?* The cards with your answers will be collected just before the program starts with a few selected for reading aloud and the others becoming possibilities for future newsletters. Thanks for sharing your wisdom!

Presentation

❖ At the beginning of the event, hand out the instructions with an index card to the participants as they arrive. Tell them, "Here's something simple you can do to contribute to tonight's program and future newsletters."

❖ At the start of the program, announce that everyone has five minutes to fill out their cards to be collected before the program begins.

❖ Gather the cards and select several to be read aloud at the close of the program.

❖ Submit all the cards to staff for publishing in future editions of the newsletter.

❖ Possible Prompts for the Question:

> If you had to pick one quality for everyone in this profession to have, what would it be and why?
>
> What about the practice of this profession are you in awe of?
>
> What is the greatest lesson you've learned from practicing this profession?
>
> About what are you unrelenting in this profession?

"Once I was introduced to the idea of rituals, I realized just how many are manifested on a regular basis, even in the corporate arena. When there is intent behind a ritual, it can become a very powerful tool to solidify teamwork and group support on projects. Because I've seen how successful they can be in the workplace, I am looking forward to applying rituals at home. Now that I have twin sons and a daughter, I plan to raise them with rituals as a way to build family values and closeness, and to help them live richer and more fulfilling lives."
       —Cindy Knowlton, Brand Marketing Executive,
                                      Boulder, Colorado

Selling Up in a Down Market

My good friend Katie used to be ritual-resistant. Now she conducts rituals. In fact, her circle of friends regularly ask her to design rituals. One of these friends asked her to design a ritual that would compel the perfect buyer to buy their home, which had been on the market for a considerable period of time. Katie gleefully took this request on—with great results. There was an acceptable offer on the table within twenty-four hours of the ritual!

This ritual is based upon the one that netted such great results for Katie's friend.

—Linda Ann Smith

Purpose

❖ Cultivating the right home buyer, at the right price in any market.

Props

❖ Votive candles, one for each person present plus an extra to serve as an anchor candle.

❖ A bundle of ritual sage (such as white sage) that can be divided, or small individual sticks of sage.

Preparation

- ❖ Offer to facilitate the ritual for a friend selling her home.
- ❖ Invite family and friends of the home seller, asking them to come prepared for a ritual to call forth the perfect home buyer.

Presentation

- ❖ Gather the group around the dinner table, asking each person to light a candle in the middle of the dinner table, where you have already placed a votive candle for each person.
- ❖ Each person lights their candle from an anchor candle, placed prominently. (In the world of candle lighting, one should only light candles for a ritual from an anchor candle.)
- ❖ Ask each person to share the following:

    What experiences you have had in this house that were fun, pleasurable, inspiring, motivating, joyful, poignant?

    What attributes does the house possess (you can do it room by room) that will bring the same bounty to the person buying the home?

❖ After the sharing, give each person a sprig or small stick of sage to light from the candle. Take the group outside and have them circle the house, shrouding it with the sage smoke. The sage will cleanse the house of all of the lingering negative energy.

Driving the Rituals

The rituals in this book presume that one person takes the lead and guides the process of the ritual. If the ritual process was compared to a car full of people taking a scenic drive, then we can say that the ritual leader is like the driver, who makes sure the other passengers can sit back and enjoy the scenery. Here are a few tips for ensuring you are effective as the driver of a ritual.

Preparation

* ❖ From the outset, be sure to explain the purpose and presentation to all the participants.
* ❖ Let the participants know if they are expected to contribute to any preparations or props, and give them plenty of time to think about their contribution.

❖ Coordinate arrangements and share tasks if you need help and doing so would enrich the occasion.

❖ Prepare simple activities for opening and closing the ritual that complement the purpose.

❖ Select and arrange objects for a ritual centerpiece.

Presentation

❖ As the participants arrive, assume the role of hostess, making it easy for everyone to relax and enjoy themselves.

❖ Ask everyone to gather. Once they are settled, share the opening activity.

❖ Take a few minutes to explain exactly what will occur during the ritual's presentation.

❖ Navigate the participants through the ritual, paying attention to the level of participation to ensure that everyone has a chance to share.

❖ Be open to unexpected, in-the-moment occurrences. Rituals create a special space for surprises to happen.

❖ When the ritual has concluded, share the closing activity and thank everyone for their contributions to the journey.

Power of Rituals

Guidelines for Creating Your Own Ritual

PURPOSE—Be specific about your reasons for creating the ritual. Who or how do you want to connect? What information or understanding do you want to cultivate? What event or person do you want to celebrate? Once the purpose is identified and articulated, it is much easier to design the ritual. Here are some questions to help you to determine your purpose:

❖ What is compelling about the event?

_____

_____

❖ What is your primary purpose for the ritual?

_____

_____

❖ For you to feel fulfilled what has to happen?

_____

_____

PREPARATION and PRESENTATION—A step-by-step process will ensure a successful and well received ritual. These questions will help you create a process for the ritual:

❖ What actions and activities during the ritual would enhance the ritual?

_____

_____

❖ How many people will be involved?

_____

_____

❖ Where and when will it take place?

_____

_____

BEGINNING THE RITUAL—Beginning a ritual can be as simple as taking a few moments for silence, reading a poem or forming a circle. The point is that you and the other participants are comfortable with the process.

❖ What ideas do you have for beginning this ritual?

_____

_____

CLOSING THE RITUAL—Closing a ritual can be as simple as opening one—and it is just as important. It is the act of affirming what you have done. You may wish to choose another reading, sing a song or break up the circle. Whatever feels right for you and the participants will work.

❖ What kind of closing will complete the ritual?

_____

_____

PROPS—You may need props to carry out the ritual. And depending on the occasion, you may need to plan refreshments.

❖ What props would you use as part of the ritual?

_____

_____

RITUAL OPTIONS TO CONSIDER—Rituals can be held in many ways. Here are just a couple of suggestions you may not have considered:

❖ Potluck Rituals—Potluck rituals (which may or may not involve food!) tap the power of the group to create the ritual. Begin by choosing an appropriate theme for the gathering. Then let the group use the same elements listed above to plan what the group will be doing. This on-the-spot ritual-making has the advantage of immediately engaging everyone, since they've had a hand in the planning.

❖ **In-The-Moment Rituals**—You may find yourself
in a situation that calls for an in-the-moment
ritual—something to celebrate or a need to bring
people together. Keep it short and sweet. Let people
know what to do and then just do it. For example,
at the beginning of a meeting at which participants
are not all known to or familiar with one another,
you can add a prompt to the typical introduction
of name and affiliation. Here are some sample
prompts:

If I weren't at this meeting, I'd be . . .

What I most appreciate about living in (your city
or state) . . .

My funniest memory of a meeting gone awry is . . .

Sharing Your Rituals

We would like to share your rituals with the world so you too can inspire people to connect, cultivate and celebrate the relationships of their lives. To share your ritual(s), go to www.PowerofRituals.com. Click on "Share Your Rituals" and follow the prompts.

Future Power of Rituals Books
For Baby Boomers
For Teens
For Women Second Edition
For Teachers
For Guys
For Athletes
For Romance
For Communities
For the Artist in You
For Families
From the Well-Known
From the Heartland
From Our Men and Women in Uniform

Power of Rituals Products can be ordered at
<u>www.PowerofRituals.com</u>:

Dinner Talk Cards©: Deck of cards with questions and beginning sentences to stories. Designed to spark conversation at the dinner table. The human soul loves to tell their stories and hear others for inspiration.

And the Question Is©: Questions to ask for a variety of occasions. Everything from what you should ask the retirement community you want to move your parents into, to questions you ask a prospective employer before accepting a job.

Write'n Hike Journal©: Designed for creative writing hikes with friends or writing clubs.

Baby Blessing Journal©: For use with the Baby Blessing Ritual in the "Celebration" chapter.

Wedding Blessings Journal©: For use with the Spa Wedding Shower ritual in the "Celebration" chapter.

StoryTelling Journal©: Capture the stories of your family, childhood friends, sorority sisters, neighbors, community.

What I Know©: Success journal for children.

Ask the
Ritual Experts

Are you turning 50? Is your Grandmother turning 90? Is your first grandchild on the way? Would you like to do something to commemorate these extraordinary moments other then a potluck dinner?

Contact Linda Ann Smith or Kelly Blair Roberts, the Ritual Experts, at www.PowerofRituals.com. Designing rituals to connect, cultivate and celebrate the relationships of your life is what we do. Consulting fees will apply.

"My co-worker and I took on the responsibility of designing a bachelorette party for another co-worker. What we knew for sure was that we wanted to celebrate her uniqueness and not do the usual hitting the bars all night. We hired Linda and Kelly to assist us in this endeavor. The result was that the bride-to-be was touched, moved and inspired and the guests were given the opportunity to celebrate their friend in a special and extraordinary way. The bachelorette party was a huge success."

—Audri Ivey

Opportunities
to Create Rituals

To Connect, Cultivate and Celebrate
the Relationships of your Life
(Recommended Rituals are in Italics)

Anniversaries...*Memories are Made of This*
Baby Showers, Births, Adoptions...*Baby Blessings*
Birthdays...*Birthday Buy the Book or Third Act or Write 'n Hike*
Chinese New Year
Cleaning out Clutter
College...Leaving for, Graduation
Conflict...*On the Road Again*
Cooking...*Passion Soup Soiree*
Divorce
Engagements
End-of-Life Passages...*Graceful Grief or Legacy of Values*
Family Dinners, Picnics
Firsts...Day of School, Date, Anything Brand New
First Day...of Winter, Spring, Summer or Fall
Friendships...Celebrating New Ones or Ending Old Ones
Garage Sales
Grandparents Day
Hikes
Holidays

Home Related...Deciding to Sell, Selling or Buying a House,
Housewarmings...
Selling Up in a Down Market or New Home Blessings
Job Related...Starting a New Job, Ending a Job, Promotions, Raises
Launching a Book
Launching a Business:...*FuturePace or What Would You Do
if You Knew You Would Succeed*
Leap Year
Medical or Surgical Experiences...*Surgical Journey or Tend & Befriend*
Moving to a New City, State or Country
Parents Moving into a Retirement Community
Proms
Rainy Days, Snowy Days, Blue Sky Days
Recovery from Illness or Loss
Resolving Conflicts
Returns of...the Prodigal Son or Daughter or
Relatives Serving in the Military
Retirements
Reunions...*Reunions are Not Always Relative or Answers
from Our Ancestors*
Romantic Gains or Losses
Sadie Hawkins Day
School Days...First Day, Last Day, Snow Days
Super Bowl Sunday
Support...for your Friends or from Your Friends
Tax Day
Teacher Appreciation Day
Teambuilding:...*Circle the Wisdom or Pearls of Wisdom*
Tooth Fairy
Transitions...*The Wrinkle Ritual or Footprints in the Sand*
Vacations...Departing, In the Moment, Returning
Wedding Day, Night, Honeymoon
Wedding Showers...*Spa Bridal Shower*